FURIOUS EUROS

FURIOUS EURO'S

THE EUROPEAN CHAMPIONSHIPS 1960-2004

MICHAEL COLEMAN

Illustrated by

Mike Phillips

Hippo

Scholastic Children's Books,
Commonwealth House, 1–19 New Oxford Street,
London WC1A 1NU, UK
A division of Scholastic Ltd
London ~ New York ~ Toronto ~ Sydney ~ Auckland
Mexico City ~ New Delhi ~ Hong Kong

First published in the UK by Scholastic Ltd, 2000
This edition (revised) published in the UK by Scholastic Ltd, 2004

Text copyright © Michael Coleman, 2004
Illustrations copyright © Mike Phillips, 2004

ISBN 0 439 97754 1

Contents

—INTRODUCTION—

Football is sometimes fantastic, sometimes fierce – and sometimes really foul! This is especially the case when different countries play against each other...

The European Championships, the tournament to find out the top team in Europe, has seen its share of the fantastic, the fierce and the foul, like...

- the *fantastic* goalscorer who was a ballerina!
- the *fierce* general who wouldn't let his team play against a country he didn't like.
- the *foul* bomb-dropping England star.

You can bet that things will be no different when the finals of the next tournament, Euro 2004, take place in June. They're being hosted by Portugal, famous for its rich port wine.

WHAT A FANTASTIC TOURNAMENT! PITY WE LOST EVERY GAME 20-0!

So which country will be toasting their success after being crowned as Euro-Champs ... and which will be drowning their sorrows after ending up as Euro-Chumps?

This book will help you assess the form. It will tell you about all the previous Euro-championships, like...

● the year the competition was dominated by an elephant and a player with an autographed leg.
● the year a whole team went to prison.

And, in the best traditions, it will confer awards on the celebrities (and the not-so-celebrated) who have made the Euro Championships special. Like...

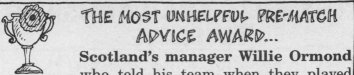

THE MOST UNHELPFUL PRE-MATCH ADVICE AWARD...

Scotland's manager Willie Ormond
– who told his team when they played Sweden in a qualifying game in 1975,

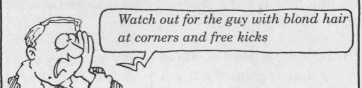

Watch out for the guy with blond hair at corners and free kicks

Good advice – except that the Swedes had six blond-headed players in their team!

BLOND! BLOND! BLOND!

So don't do a Eu-turn. Read on!

THE EURO CHAMPIONSHIPS TIMELINE

Football matches between countries began over 125 years ago – with the meeting of two countries who are still hoping to be crowned official Euro-Champs one day...

1872 England play Scotland in the first ever international football match. It's a 0-0 draw! Even so, the two teams carry on meeting each other.

1876 Wales join in, but not very well. Scotland beat them 4-0.

1882 Northern Ireland join in – and don't feel well! They lose 13-0 to England!

1883 Where football is concerned England, Scotland, Wales and Northern Ireland think they're in a league of their own. To prove it they set up a league of their own. It's modestly called the International Championship and the first winners are ... Scotland!

1902 Austria beat Hungary 5-0 in the first European international match to take place outside Britain.

Realizing they're no longer alone, England & Co. change the name of their tournament to the *Home* International Championship.

1924 Scandinavian countries Denmark, Finland, Norway and Sweden begin their own version of the Home International Championship. No, it's not called the Away International Championship, it's called the Nordic Cup.

1927 A similar championship starts with Austria, Czechoslovakia, Hungary, Italy and Switzerland taking part.

Question: What was it called?

● The Nations Cup.
● The International Cup.
● The Europe Cup.
● The Dr Gero Cup.

Answer: All of them. The competition changed its name over the years.

1927 Frenchman, Henri Delaunay, suggests that instead of having all these different competitions it would be better to have just one championship to find the

11

best international team in the whole of Europe. Nobody takes any notice of him.

1954 UEFA (pronounced *You-Ay-Far*), the Union of European Football Associations, is formed. It's a committee to organize all the football competitions in Europe and Henri Delaunay becomes its Secretary. UEFA's first job? Think of some European competitions to organize!

1955 Henri Delaunay dies. His son Pierre reminds everybody of Henri's suggestion in 1927 about an International European Championship. A-ha! Just the thing for UEFA to organize!

1958 5 April. The first European Championship gets under way. Except that it's not called that; it's called the European Nations Cup.

WHY DIDN'T THEY CALL IT THE FOOTBALL ASSOCIATIONS' BROTHERHOOD? THAT WOULD HAVE BEEN FAB!

AND EASIER TO PRONOUNCE!

THE MOST UNKNOWN TROPHY NAME AWARD...
The trophy being played for during Euro 2004. It's called (and has been ever since 1958) the Henri Delaunay Cup, in memory of the man who first had the idea.

1968 The tournament is renamed. From now on it's known by its official title of the European Championship.

1996 The finals get a nickname. Played in England, they're simply known as Euro '96.

2000 The nickname changes. The finals are called Euro 2000 – presumably because it's too tricky to say EURO-Oh-Oh!

2004 With youngsters everywhere being encouraged to improve their fitness by giving up junk food and fizzy drinks, and spend less time watching TV and talking on their mobile phones, the sponsors for Euro 2004 are announced. They include a fast-food chain, a fizzy-drinks producer, a TV manufacturer and a mobile-phone company.

The Euro 2004 tournament will be the twelfth European Championships to be played. How have the previous Euro tournaments gone? Have the matches always been eulogized? Have the winners always been euphoric?

Euro-bout to find out!

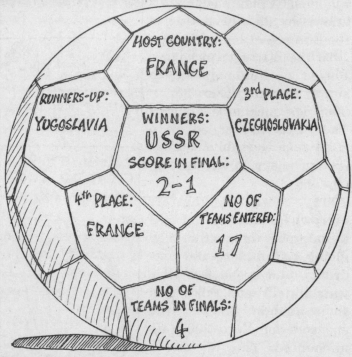

HOST COUNTRY:
FRANCE

RUNNERS-UP:
YUGOSLAVIA

WINNERS:
USSR
SCORE IN FINAL:
2-1

3rd PLACE:
CZECHOSLOVAKIA

4th PLACE:
FRANCE

NO OF
TEAMS ENTERED:
17

NO OF
TEAMS IN FINALS:
4

Who's playing, then?

To reach the finals of Euro 2004, countries will have had to fight their way through qualifying rounds starting way back in 2002. It was no different the first time the competition was played. Right from the start the European Championships were designed to fit into the four-year gap between World Cups, and take two years to complete. Euro '60 actually began on 5 April 1958.

But which countries took part? In 1930, when the first ever World Cup tournament kicked off, the top footballing countries of England, Italy, Germany and Holland had been too snooty to take part. They only joined in later, once the competition had proved to be successful.

Furious Euro's question
So, nearly thirty years older and wiser, which of these countries paid their entry fee of £50 and joined in with Euro '60?
Answer: None of them! They all stayed away again, saying that the competition wouldn't catch on.

First out of the hat!
Euro '60 was designed to be a knockout competition. In the first and second rounds teams would play home and away legs, with the aggregate score (a posh way of saying the scores of the two games added together) deciding the winner.

I'VE BEEN PLAYING HOME AND AWAY LEGS FOR YEARS!

WOOF!

But a knockout competition needs 16 teams – and 17 had entered! So how was the problem solved? By picking two countries to play a preliminary match to

15

knock the number down to 16.

Eire (the Republic of Ireland) and Czechoslovakia were the unlucky pair, with Eire losing 4-2 on aggregate to gain the doubtful honour of being the first team to be knocked out of the European Championships!

EIRE WE GO OUT, EIRE WE GO OUT, EIRE WE GO OUT...

Another bad draw

The draw then took place for the 16-team first round proper. For Euro 2004 this was a swish affair with TV cameras and stacks of newspaper reporters. But the draw for Euro '60 hardly got a mention. The organizers made the mistake of holding the ceremony in Sweden during the 1958 World Cup Finals – and all the cameras and reporters were too busy watching the matches and going to World Cup events. Hardly anybody turned up to watch the Euro '60 draw!

NO. 16

'60

I DON'T THINK MUCH OF THIS BINGO CALLER

Big crowds, little crowds

Some of the Euro '60 matches had spectator problems as well. For their first-round match against Hungary, the Soviet Union (USSR) played in front of a packed crowd of 100,572! But when they won their second-round game against Spain it was in front of ... er ... 0 fans!

How come?

There was no game for them to watch! The Spaniards didn't turn up! The dictator of Spain, General Franco, wouldn't let them go to Russia. He was still sore because the Soviet Union had sent troops to fight against him in the Spanish Civil War 25 years before!

This didn't bother the Russians. UEFA had to award them a walk-over so they simply said, "Franco very much!" and went through to the final tournament in France.

Furious Euro's question
The Euro 2004 finals will last for over three weeks. How long did the Euro '60 finals last?
Answer: Five days! This was because they only included the semi-finals, a third place match, and the final. The worst you could do was come fourth!

The first Euro-Champs

What's more, the host country – France – hadn't been chosen years before as the hosts are now. Until Euro '80 the rule was that the host country was chosen from one of the four semi-finalists (France, Yugoslavia, Czechoslovakia and Hungary), to make it more likely that bigger crowds would turn up to watch the games. This was a good idea – but picking France wasn't. Over 26,000 turned up to see them play Yugoslavia in the semi-final but, after they were beaten 5-4, most of them said *au revoir* and only a miserable 9,500 fans turned up to watch the third place match against Czechoslovakia. (And were *très* disappointed. France lost that one too, 2-0.)

The final didn't do much better. Compared to the 50,000 who sat in comfort and watched the Euro 2000 final, a mouldy 18,000 saw the USSR (who'd beaten Czechoslovakia 3-0 in their semi-final) beat Yugoslavia 2-1 to become the first ever Euro-Champs.

In spite of this the tournament had been a reasonable success and the countries like England who'd stayed away were kicking themselves. Well, one Englishman wasn't...

> **THE ONLY ENGLISHMAN TO PERFORM IN A EURO-FINAL AWARD...**
> **Arthur Ellis.** Who did he play for? Nobody. English referee Arthur Ellis was in charge of the final.

Walk-outs and wars

Spain's non-appearance against the USSR isn't the only disappearing act in the history of the competition. Try this mini-quiz and see if you find it a walk-over...

1 In the Euro '64 series, little Albania were given a walk-over into the second round because their opponents, Greece, refused to travel to Albania. Why?
a) They didn't think the Albanian airport was safe.
b) They were officially at war with Albania.
c) The Albanians refused to tell them where the ground was.

...WELL, IS IT NEAR THE CITY CENTRE? I'M NOT TELLING!

2 The Yugoslavian team weren't allowed to take part in the Euro '92 final tournament. What had they done wrong?

a) They hadn't qualified properly.

b) They'd been found guilty of bribing a referee during a qualifying match.

c) Nothing.

3 During qualification for Euro '84, Malta were banned – but allowed to carry on playing. What was the problem?

a) None of their pitches were good enough for international football; they were allowed to carry on after finding a pitch outside Malta.

b) One of their players wasn't Maltese; they were allowed to carry on if they left him out.

c) Their shirts were the wrong colour; they were allowed to carry on after buying a new set.

Answers:

1b) The two countries were still officially fighting their own little bit of the Balkans War – and had been since 1912!

2c) At least, the footballers had done nothing wrong. The team had qualified properly and come top of their group. But when war broke out between Bosnia, Croatia and Serbia (the three parts of Yugoslavia) the world's politicians decided that Serbia had to be punished – and disqualification  from Euro '92 for Yugoslavia was part of the package. Talk about a penalty!

3a) After complaints from visiting teams that they were being given a bumpy ride, Malta were only allowed to stay in the competition if they played all their "home" games somewhere other than Malta. In the end, they made a profit – one of their group opponents, Holland, paid Malta £20,000 to stage their "home" match against them in Holland instead of a neutral country!

I CAN'T RUN UP HILL ANY MORE!

HOST COUNTRY:
SPAIN

RUNNERS-UP:
USSR

WINNERS:
SPAIN

3rd PLACE:
HUNGARY

SCORE IN FINAL:
2 - 1

4th PLACE:
DENMARK

NO. OF
TEAMS ENTERED:
29

NO. OF
TEAMS IN FINAL:
4

We want to play, now...

By the time Euro '64 came along quite a few countries
had changed their mind about the competition. In
fact, all but four of the possible 33 European countries
decided to take part in Euro '64. Which out of the
following were the four who stayed away?

CYPRUS · WEST GERMANY · SCOTLAND · FINLAND · ENGLAND · ITALY · HOLLAND

Answer: Cyprus, Finland, Scotland and West Germany. After seeing how wrong they were about Euro '60, England, Holland and Italy now wanted to play!

... even if we're no good!

None of them did very well, though. Italy and Holland were both knocked out in the second round, Italy by the USSR and Holland by little Luxemburg! As for England, they didn't even get that far. France whacked them 6-3 on aggregate in the first round!

WAS IT WORTH US UNPACKING?

THE WORST START FOR A WORLD-BEATING MANAGER AWARD...

Sir Alf Ramsey who, in his first appearance as England manager on 27 February 1963 saw France beat his team 5-2 in the second leg of their Euro '64 first round match. Three years later he was still in charge, but this time of a more successful England team – they won the World Cup!

I'm home!

Euro '64 saw some of the little countries doing well. Northern Ireland, for instance, beat Poland 4-0 in the first round with one of their goals scored by John Crossan – a player who'd been banned from playing in the UK for three years because he'd accepted money to join a club while still an amateur player. Was he happy about this? Of course not – he was really Cross-an!

We give in! Well, maybe not...
By far the biggest surprise of the competition was the second-round giant-killing of Holland by titchy little Luxemburg, 3-2 on aggregate. (They hadn't giant-killed anybody in the first round: they'd been one of three countries given a bye!)

Holland were certainly surprised – they usually put out their reserve team whenever they played useless Luxemburg!

As for Luxemburg themselves, they were absolutely amazed! They'd been so certain they were going to lose that they'd agreed to give up their home game and get extra money by playing both legs of the tie in Holland!

All good things must come to an end...
Luxembourg didn't make it to the finals. They were knocked out in the quarter-finals by Denmark who, along with Spain, Hungary and the USSR, made up the four semi-finalists. Again the host country was chosen from one of these four – and this time UEFA

got it right! They picked Spain as host country and the Spaniards duly won their way to the final ... and a match against the USSR, the team General Franco had forbidden them to play in Euro '60!

Furious Euro's question
What did General Franco do in Euro '64?
Answer: He turned up (along with 119,999 other spectators) to watch the match!

It was a good decision. In pouring rain, Spain won 2-1 to become Euro '64 Champions. It was the USSR's first ever defeat in the competition.

I THOUGHT THE RAIN IN SPAIN STAYED MAINLY ON THE PLAIN!

Euro Star: Lev Yashin

Why was the USSR goalkeeper Lev Yashin like a fast train? Because, as a member of both their Euro '60 and Euro '64 teams, he was a real Euro Star! And yet he might not have been a footballer at all...

Yashin joined his club, Moscow Dynamo, as a

17-year-old goalkeeper. Not to play football, though – he joined as an ice-hockey goalkeeper! Dynamo had teams in both sports and Yashin played the icy game until they discovered he could skate across a muddy goalmouth just as well.

Even so, he almost gave up football to concentrate on ice-hockey. After two seasons stuck in Dynamo's reserve team, and getting only the occasional first-team game, Lev was about to hang up his football boots and pull on his skates when, aged 24, an injury to the regular goalkeeper gave him his chance to be the No. 1 choice. It was a chance Lev grabbed with both giant hands, playing so well for the first team they couldn't "lev" him out again! Yashin stayed as Dynamo's goalkeeper for 17 years, finally retiring when he was 41 years old.

Nowadays, with goalkeepers looking like explosions in a paint factory, Lev Yashin would have looked very boring. He dressed in black – all over! Black jersey, black shorts, black socks. No surprise, then, that the colour figured as part of his nickname...

Question: What was his nickname?

THE BLACK OCTOPUS

THE BLACK SPIDER

THE BLACK PANTHER

Answer: All of them. South American opponents called him "spider" and Europeans called him "octopus" or "panther" – presumably because to them he seemed to have eight arms, six legs and the agility of a big cat!

But then who wouldn't have thought that of a goalkeeper who saved over 150 penalties during his career!

There was one non-black part to Lev Yashin's goalkeeping outfits: his caps. He always took *two* on to the pitch. One he wore on his head, of course.

Furious Euro's question
What did he do with the other cap? **Answer:** He put it in the back of his net for luck. (Which just shows that footballers can be superstitious even when they're as cap-able as Yashin!)

The cap for his head had more than one use as well. In 1958, when the USSR played England in a

World Cup group match, England were awarded a doubtful penalty. To show his disgust at the decision, Yashin yanked off his cap – and threw it at the referee!

That 1958 World Cup tournament was the first of four that Lev appeared in. He also played in the 1962 and 1966 competitions (in Chile and England) and, aged 41, went to Mexico in 1970 as the USSR's reserve goalkeeper.

During the 1962 World Cup Lev Yashin proved that even super stars have days when they play more like falling stars. In Russia's match against Colombia, the Colombians won a corner. The ball came swinging over, Yashin went out to meet it – and missed it altogether! The ball went straight into the net.

Usually, though, players were nothing short of amazed if they ever did score against Yashin. In the same 1962 World Cup, the Chilean player Eladio Rojas was so delighted at scoring from 25 metres out that he raced all the way up to the unhappy goalkeeper and gave him a big "thank you" hug!

During his career he played for his country 78 times, winning a gold medal with the 1956 Olympic football team to go with his Euro '60 winner's and Euro '64 loser's medals.

To date, Lev Yashin is the only goalkeeper to have been voted (in 1963) European Footballer of the Year.

Yep, when it came to keeping, Yashin was smashin'!

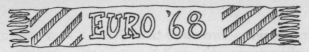

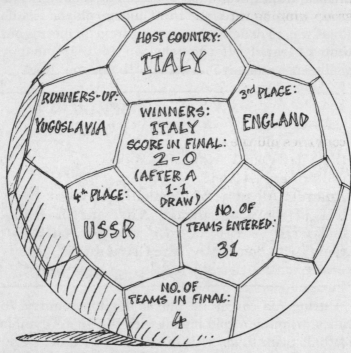

HOST COUNTRY:
ITALY

RUNNERS-UP:
YUGOSLAVIA

WINNERS:
ITALY
SCORE IN FINAL:
2-0
(AFTER A
1-1
DRAW)

3rd PLACE:
ENGLAND

4th PLACE:
USSR

NO. OF
TEAMS ENTERED:
31

NO. OF
TEAMS IN FINAL:
4

Knockout knocked out!

There were a couple of changes made for Euro '68. One was the name of the competition itself. Instead of the European Nations Cup it was changed to the name it now has: the European Championship.

The other change did away with the early rounds of the competition being played on a knockout basis. Instead UEFA decided to copy the World Cup and introduced qualifying groups. Just as they are today, these groups were played as mini-leagues with each team meeting the others twice, once at home and once away.

The 31 countries – two more than Euro '64 – were divided into eight groups, with the top team in each group winning through to the quarter-finals.

Fancy meeting you here!

Furious Euro's question
For the first time, Scotland were taking part. Which other home countries did they have along with them in Group 8 – England, Wales or Northern Ireland?
Answer: All three of them! It wasn't the (bad) luck of the draw, though. The four countries had asked for it to be that way. It meant they could play for their own Home International Championship at the same time – which they still thought was more important!

SO WE ALL AGREE, WE'RE NOT GOING TO LET A LITTLE THING LIKE THE EUROPEAN CHAMPIONSHIP STOP US FROM KICKING THE HELL OUT OF EACH OTHER?

The new world champions!
In the end, England came top of the group. Not that Scotland cared very much. They got what they wanted by beating England (the reigning world champions after winning the World Cup in 1966)

31

3-2 at Wembley in their group match. To the Scottish newspapers that meant only one thing: Scotland were now world champions!

THE DAILY SPORRAN

SCOTLAND 3 ENGLAND 2
WEE ARE THE CHAMPIONS!
We made porridge out of them!

Plenty in reserve!
The Republic of Ireland came up with an unlikely star during their group matches. Injuries left them short of players before their match against Czechoslovakia. So they were forced to call up Turloch O'Connor, a striker so unknown that only five days before he'd been playing for Fulham reserves!

It all worked out well in the end, though. They won the game 2-1, and O'Connor scored the winner!

THE CRAFTIEST PRE-MATCH TACTIC AWARD...
The Czechoslovakian Brass Band, who, before their country's group match against Spain, played the wrong Spanish national anthem! The Czechs went on to win the game 1-0, but Spain still came top of the group.

Be prepared!

Spain were then beaten by England, giving the English a place (along with Yugoslavia, USSR and Italy) in the final knockout tournament to be played in Italy. For their semi-final match England were drawn against Yugoslavia.

Question: How did they prepare for such an important game?

a) They travelled to Italy a week before the game and practised hard.

b) They travelled to Italy two weeks before and practised incredibly hard.

c) They played a friendly four days before the semi-final and then travelled to Italy where they hardly practised at all.

Answer: c) Over-confident England played a friendly against West Germany, and then travelled to Italy to face Yugoslavia ... where they lost, 0-1.

The Yugoslavian goal was scored by their tricky left winger, Dragan Dzajic. He scorched his way past the England defenders so often that the newspapers nicknamed him "The Magic Dragan"!

Their only consolation was that they then beat the USSR 2-0 to grab third place.

Ready, steady – goal!

The Italians' luck held out all the way through to the end of the tournament. In the final, they were losing 1-0 to Yugoslavia when they got a free kick on the edge of the Yugolsav's penalty area...

What happened next?

Answer: As the referee was pushing the defensive wall back, Italy's midfielder Domenghini took the kick – while most of the Yugoslav defenders weren't looking! Their striker, Musemic was just about the only person in the wall who saw what was happening. And what did he do when he saw the ball heading his way? He ducked! Domenghini's shot whistled into the net – and, to everybody's amazement, the referee whistled for a goal!

The match ended 1-1, and Italy won the replay 2-0 to become Euro '68 champions.

The red card quiz

Think you could keep your head when everything's going wrong? When you're being punched and kicked and fouled by the foulest fouler who ever fouled? If so, you'll be a lot better than these players: they all got sent off during European Championship matches. Try this red card quiz – but if you get them all wrong, don't see red!

1 Alan Mullery was the first ever England player to be sent off during an international match. It happened in the Euro '68 semi-final against Yugoslavia. Trivic of Yugoslavia fouled Mullery, who promptly kicked him back – and Trivic's leg was broken. True or false?

2 The first tournament, Euro '60, saw a sending-off in the second-round match between Italy and the USSR when Pascutti (Italy) retaliated after being brought down by Dubinski (USSR). What did the Italian do to the Soviet player?

a) He head-butted him.
b) He kissed him on both cheeks.
c) He swapped shirts with him.

35

3 In a Euro '80 qualifying game, Byron Stephenson of Wales was sent off for fouling Mustapha of Turkey, who was injured enough to have to be substituted. And yet Turkey managed to keep Mustapha on the pitch! How did they manage it?

4 During a Euro '84 match between France and Denmark, Amoros (France) was fouled by Olsen (Denmark). Picking up the ball, the Frenchman threw it, hitting Olsen on the head – and was sent off for it. True or false?

5 When Holland beat the Czech Republic with a disputed penalty during their group match in Euro 2000, Radoslav Latal argued so much that he was sent off – even though he wasn't on the pitch. Was rowdy Radoslav...
a) The Czech's coach.
b) A Czech player.
c) The Czech's coach driver.

6 In the Euro '92 qualifying group match between Italy and Norway, Bergomi of Italy was sent off for two yellow cards: the first for a foul on Lydersen and then, in the last minute of the game, for a foul on Sorloth. What was so amazing about Bergomi's performance?
a) He hadn't touched the ball once.
b) It was the first time he'd ever been sent off.
c) He was playing his first game for Italy.

Answers:

1 False. Mullery did kick Trivic, but he certainly didn't break his leg. The Yugoslav simply acted as though he had, rolling around in agony under the referee's nose. Once Mullery had left the pitch Trivic jumped up again! (And was fit enough to play in the final *and* the replay!)

2a) with a bit of **c)** Pascutti not only head-butted

3 By replacing Mustapha (known as Mustapha One) by his namesake, known as Mustapha Two!

THEY MUSTAPHA LOT OF THESE!

MUSTAPHA

MUSTAPHA

4 False. The ball missed. Unfortunately Amoros then made up for it by deciding to head-butt Olsen instead. *That's* what he got sent off for!

5b) Latal was a midfield player who'd been substituted. He was red-carded for raging at the fourth official on the touchline.

6a) Bergomi was the Italians' substitute, and he'd only come on in the 89th minute, when the Italians were losing 2-1. He immediately committed foul number one and then, a couple of minutes later and before he'd even touched the ball, he was sent off for his second foul!

Euro Battles 1: England v. Scotland

Why was beating England in the Euro '68 qualifying round more important to Scotland than actually reaching the finals? Because the two countries have been "enemies" ever since international football began. The English always want to "scotch" the Scots' plans and Scotland always want to mangle the "Auld Enemy" as England are known.

Every match between the two countries over the years has been a big battle. Here's a run-down on the biggest of them.

1872–4 The first three games set the scene. The first is drawn (0-0) and then the countries win one each (England 4-2 in 1873, Scotland 2-1 in 1874). Each of these early games was a battle of tactics because the two countries played in an entirely different way. Here's how you did it if you were an England player and got the ball:

 ① Try to beat the first Scottish player you come to...

 ② If you succeed, try to beat the next Scottish player you come to...

③ Keep beating Scottish players until there's none left...

④ Kick the ball in the goal!

BOOT!

If you lost the ball and it went to one of the other English players, then they would do exactly the same thing.

If you were a Scot, though, it was different. This is what you would do if you got the ball:

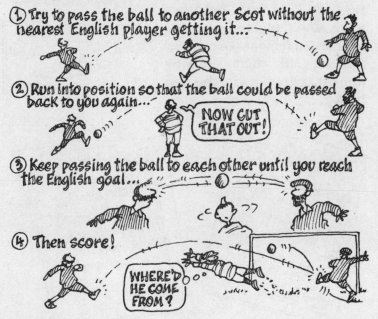

① Try to pass the ball to another Scot without the nearest English player getting it...

② Run into position so that the ball could be passed back to you again...

NOW CUT THAT OUT!

③ Keep passing the ball to each other until you reach the English goal...

④ Then score!

WHERE'D HE COME FROM?

That's how it was. For many years the English played a "dribbling" game, and the Scots played a "passing" game, until...

1928 The Scots turn up at Wembley and win 5-1 with one of the most brilliant displays of passing ever seen – so brilliant that, afterwards, the Scottish team were dubbed "The Wembley Wizards". And yet the English fans had laughed when they saw them run out, because the tallest of the Scots forwards was 5ft 7" (1.7m)! But they were soon laughing at their own defenders as the Scots' passing left them chasing around trying to win the ball back.

Sunday Chronicle

"Never was a country more humiliated on its own soil!"

Daily Mirror

"England were not beaten at Wembley. They were routed and outpaced and thrashed"

1955 England change their style and finally get their own back. The Scots come to Wembley and are whacked 7-2! The star of the English team is tricky winger Stanley Matthews – who's 40 years young!

STAN THE MAN

THE MOST OPTIMISTIC THINKING AWARD...

The 1955 Scots team. Two years before, England had lost to the famous "Magic Magyars" of Hungary 6-3 in their first defeat by a foreign side at Wembley. Playing Hungary themselves not long after, Scotland lost 4-2. As that wasn't as bad as losing 6-3 the Scots reckoned they must be better than England!

1961 England carry on getting their own back. They beat the Scots at Wembley 9-3! The unfortunate Scots' goalkeeper is playing only his second game for his country – and, not surprisingly, it's also his last. His name is Frank Haffey, and the poor bloke immediately features in endless rotten jokes. Like:

HEY, HAFFEY, YOU DROPPED YOUR CAP. HERE, CATCH!

Frank, how did you feel about letting in nine goals? I wasn't very Haffey about it!

41

What's the time in England?
Nearly ten past Haffey!

What song did the England players sing in the bath?
Haffey days are here again!

HA! HA! HA! HOO! HOO! HEE! HEE!

Sunday Express

This was slaughter in the spring sunshine.

A *misled public and the Scottish press ridiculously laid all the blame on Haffey. I reckon any goalkeeper would have been jittery behind that defence!*

ENGLAND'S STAR FORWARD

JIMMY GREAVES

THE MOST AGONIZINGLY AWFUL PRESENT FOR A SCOTLAND SUPPORTER AWARD...
    A long-playing record released not long after the 9-3 defeat by England. It had the complete radio commentary of the match on it!

1967 Scotland beat World Cup winners England 3-2 at Wembley and proclaim themselves World Champions! The Scots fans are so delirious with joy they run on to the Wembley pitch and start digging bits up to take home as souvenirs. How do we know it was the Scots fans and not the English? Because the centre spot turned up in Glasgow a week later!

1977 Another Scottish win at Wembley (by 2-1, with Scots hero Kenny Dalglish scoring the winning goal) and another pitch invasion. But by now, Wembley is equipped with an electronic scoreboard. Up flashes the message: "In the interests of safety please slowly clear the pitch".

Unfortunately many of the drunken invaders take the advice to heart – and start to clear the pitch of everything on it! Both goals are smashed and the pitch has huge lumps dug out of it again. In all, 132 fans were arrested and appeared in court the next week...

THE WORST EXCUSE FROM A FOOTBALL HOOLIGAN AWARD...

The Scots fan who really did appear in front of the magistrates at Bow Street court after being arrested for pitch-stealing. He tried to excuse what he did by saying,

> *The turf was from the spot where Kenny Dalglish scored the winning goal. I was going to take it home and put it in a jar on my mantelpiece and just watch it grow and remember the match*

1981 Not wanting Wembley wrecked again (even though the Scottish FA had bought them a new set of goalposts) the English FA refuse to sell tickets to Scottish fans. The Scottish Supporters' Club take the FA to court arguing racial discrimination – that they're being picked on simply because they're Scots, and that if they were Irish or Welsh they'd be allowed in. The judge throws out their case. (He clearly thought that the fans should pay for what they'd done before and shouldn't be allowed to get off scot-free!) Scotland have the

45

last laugh, though: even without supporters they win the match 1-0!

1984 The final game between the two countries as part of the Home International Championship, which is being scrapped. The match ends just as the first contest did, in a draw (1-1). For the next few years, England and Scotland don't let Wales or Northern Ireland play with them any more. They just play against each other for a trophy called The Rous Cup (named after Sir Stanley Rous, a former Secretary of the FA and President of FIFA).

1989 England win 2-0 in the final Rous Cup match. From now on they'll only rouse themselves to play each other when they're drawn together in the World Cup or the European Championship.

1996 They're drawn together! It happens during the first round of Euro '96 and England win 2-0 at Wembley. The most miserable Scot in the world is Gary McAllister

who misses a penalty when his team are only 1-0 down.

Question: How did England goalkeeper David Seaman save it?

a) with his left elbow

b) with his bum

c) with his right knee

Answer: a) When McAllister hit the ball straight at him. Afterwards the Scot moaned, *"Hitting it straight is not something I usually do but given the stage of the game I felt I had to score."*

1999 They're drawn together again! After finishing second in their different qualifying groups, England and Scotland are pitted against each other in a play-off match to decide which of them will go to the Euro 2000 finals and which will stay at home.

Question: The match lasts for 180 minutes instead of the usual 90. Why?

a) the referee's watch stops

b) there are an awful lot of injuries

c) it's a two-leg match

Answer: c) England win 2-0 in Scotland, and Scotland win

1-0 in England. Result: England scrape through 2-1 on aggregate.

Just as he had in 1996, England's goalkeeper David Seaman again foiled the Scots in the match at Wembley. With Scotland 1-0 ahead, he made a great save to stop them scoring a second goal and taking the match into extra-time.

Question: Who produced the goal-bound header he saved?

a) Gary McAllister

b) Christian Dailly

Answer: b) It couldn't have been Gary McAllister because he wasn't playing, even though manager Craig Brown wanted him in his team. McAllister had been booed so much by the Scots fans since missing the 1996 penalty that he'd decided never to play for his country again.

2000+ When will the old enemies meet again? World Cup 2006? Euro 2008? Who knows? Until then the record between the two countries stands at:

ENGLAND V SCOTLAND

ENGLAND 45 VICTORIES
AND 192 GOALS SCORED

SCOTLAND 41 VICTORIES
AND 169 GOALS SCORED

DRAWN BATTLES 20

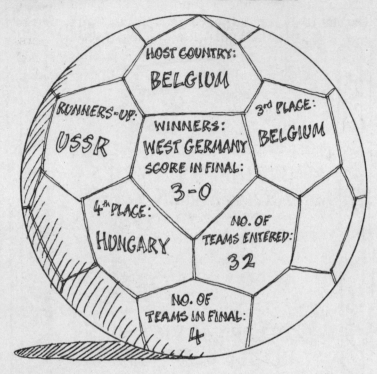

EURO '72

HOST COUNTRY:
BELGIUM

RUNNERS-UP:
USSR

WINNERS:
WEST GERMANY
SCORE IN FINAL:
3-0

3rd PLACE:
BELGIUM

4th PLACE:
HUNGARY

NO. OF
TEAMS ENTERED:
32

NO. OF
TEAMS IN FINAL:
4

Czech-mate!

Czechoslovakia were one of the favourites to win Euro '72, which was bad news for Wales because they'd been drawn in the same qualifying group. But when the Czech FA banned a lot of their own star players for taking illegal payments and could only manage to draw with tiny Finland, Wales fancied their chances.

What happened? The Czech FA decided that the prospect of losing to Wales was so completely awful they un-banned their stars – and Wales were beaten 3-1!

Wales 0 Clubs 1

Wales also lost their second-leg match against the Czechs (0-1) ... and, once again, they were able to argue that it was all the fault of banned players. This time, though, the banned players were Welsh! Their clubs had told them they weren't allowed to play for their country.

Why not? Because the Euro-match took place on the same day as the fourth round of the Football League Cup and the clubs involved wanted their top Welsh players playing for them!

THE DRIPPIEST MANAGER AND PLAYER AWARD...

Shared by Celtic and Scotland player **Kenny Dalglish** and his manager **Jock Stein**. Celtic were relaxing at their hotel in Malta before a European Cup game when Stein was telephoned to say that Dalglish had been selected for the Scots pool of players for his first international game. Off he went to find Dalglish.

KENNY! YOU'RE IN THE POOL!

I KNOW!

Stein had found him paddling in the hotel's swimming pool!

(Even with the dazzling Dalglish Scotland didn't qualify for the Euro '72 finals. Their pool of players leaked too many goals!)

England 0 Clubs 1

It wasn't only the Welsh who were affected by this sort of ban. The clubs wouldn't let their players turn out for England either, insisting that the League Cup was more important than the European Championship!

So when England played Switzerland on the same day as the fifth round of the League Cup, half their usual side were missing. They managed to scrape a 1-1 draw, though, and went through to the next round...

Give me the ball – please!

...mainly because they were in a pretty easy qualifying group. How easy? Well, Malta were one of their opponents. When England beat them 5-0 at Wembley, England's goalkeeper Gordon Banks didn't receive the ball from a Maltese player once in the whole 90 minutes. He didn't even have to take a goal-kick! He must have thought it was a Banks holiday!

SHOULDN'T HE HAVE LEFT LAST NIGHT?

When I want your autograph, I'll ask for it!

England went out in the next round, though – even with a player ban working in their favour. They were drawn against West Germany and, in the first-leg match at Wembley, the German team were missing a number of players who'd been banned after a big bribery scandal in which four German league matches were proved to have been fixed.

It didn't make any difference. The new players performed brilliantly and England were beaten 3-1. It was a game to forget, especially for World Cup hero Geoff Hurst. He was substituted, and never played for England again.

One of the German stars that night was midfield man Gunther Netzer who had been on the end of some foul tackling. After the game he said,

With the return game in Germany being drawn 0-0, England went out.

Mauled by Müller

West Germany then beat the USSR 3-0 in the final to become Euro '72 Champions. Two of their goals were scored by their ace striker Gerd Müller. That was no surprise at all. During the whole of the Euro '72 competition, West Germany had scored 18 goals – and Müller had grabbed 11 of them!

Euro Stars: Germany's goal-machines

When it comes to football, Germany are easily the most successful Euro-nation. Their win in Euro '72 proved to be the first of three triumphs so far, Euro '80 and Euro '96 being the other two. They've also been runners-up twice, in Euro '76 and Euro '92.

THE MOST SUCCESSFUL HALF-COUNTRY AWARD...

West Germany. After the Second World War, Germany was divided into two countries, East and West, staying that way until 1990. The wins at Euro '72 and Euro '80 were managed by West Germany on their own!

How do they do it? Well, for a start, by finding strikers who are worth their weight in goals! Meet three of their all-time greats...

Karl-Heinz Rummenigge

Rummenigge starred in the Euro '80 team. He played for West Germany's top club, Bayern Munich, and was twice voted European Player of the Year.

How much did Bayern pay for him in 1974?

Answer: £4,500! Ten years later he was sold to Italian club Internazionale for £2,000,000!

Rummenigge became captain of his country, but

his winning ways in the European Championships weren't matched in the World Cup. He twice led his team to the final (in 1982 and 1986) but lost them both.

He was a gentleman, though – as you'd expect from somebody who'd once been a bank clerk. Before the 1982 World Cup Final Rummenigge was injured and the West German manager, Jupp Derwall, took a big chance in putting him in the team. It was a decision that another German player, Uli Stielike, moaned about so much that he made Rummenigge mad enough to want to punch him. He didn't, though – he asked a team-mate to do it instead!

LOOK OUT FOR THAT RIGHT CROSS!

Jurgen Klinsmann

Klinsmann was Germany's star striker in Euro '92 and Euro '96 as well as playing for West Germany's less successful team in Euro '88. He managed to score goals in each tournament, making him the only player so far to have scored in three separate Euro Championships. As if that wasn't enough, Klinsmann also won a World Cup winner's medal with West Germany in 1990.

He doesn't get travel-sickness, that's for sure. In his career, Klinsmann has played for clubs in Germany (three times), Italy (twice), France and England (twice)!

His two spells in England were with Tottenham Hotspur, where he perfected one of the daftest goal-scorers' celebrations of all time.

(HEALTH WARNING: do not try to copy this trick in the playground!)

HE'D BANG THE BALL IN THE NET, THEN...

RACE MADLY TOWARDS THE TOUCHLINE, THEN...

DIVE FULL-LENGTH ON THE GRASS...

SLIDING ON HIS FRONT AS FAR AS HE COULD!

Why did he do it? Because he was trying to prove that Germans do have a sense of humour. He knew that a lot of English fans thought he was a "diver" (a forward who'd fall over if a defender breathed on him heavily, in the hope of getting a penalty) and his goal celebration was making fun of this reputation.

THE BEST-EDUCATED INTERNATIONAL FOOTBALLER AWARD...

Jurgen Klinsmann, who once said, "I swear a lot. But the advantage is that having played abroad, I can choose a different language to the referee's."

WHAT WAS THAT?

JUST SAYING WHAT A GREAT DECISION THAT WAS, REF!

Whatever the cause of his diving, Klinsmann certainly scored a lot of goals. His tally of 47 in 108 internationals makes him equal second highest goalscorer for Germany, beaten only by...

Gerd Müller

Müller was the German goal machine! He scored an incredible 68 goals in only 62 internationals. And yet he really didn't look like a footballer at all. Whereas both Rummenigge and Klinsmann were tall and slim, Müller was short and dumpy. Even his manager was fooled by his appearance...

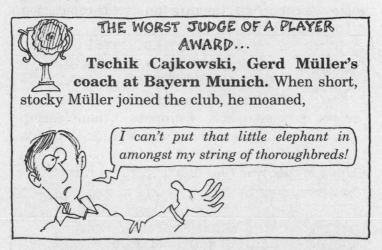

THE WORST JUDGE OF A PLAYER AWARD...
Tschik Cajkowski, Gerd Müller's coach at Bayern Munich. When short, stocky Müller joined the club, he moaned,

I can't put that little elephant in amongst my string of thoroughbreds!

Cajkowski soon ate his words, though. With Müller in their side, Bayern won three consecutive European Cups (in 1974, '75 and '76) and Müller himself went on to score an amazing 365 goals (in 427 games) in the Bundesliga, the German football league.

Here's another hat trick of facts about Müller the Magnificent:

• He had at least two nicknames: opposing fans called him "fatty" – but his own supporters called him *Der Bomber* – the Bomber – because of all the goals he blasted for club and country!

HEY! FATTY BOMB BOMB!

• One of his most important goals for Germany was in 1974,

when he scored the winning goal in the World Cup Final.

- He was the first German to win the European Footballer of the Year award, in 1970.

THE BEST SURNAME FOR A GERMAN FOOTBALLER AWARD...

Müller! Germany fielded three of them in consecutive European Championship finals. Gerd Müller scored and won in Euro '72, Deiter Müller scored (but lost) in Euro '76 and Hans Müller won (but didn't score) in Euro '80.

THE WORST FIRST NAME FOR A GERMAN FOOTBALLER AWARD...

Ludwig. How else can you explain West Germany's failure to qualify for Euro '68, even though they had Ludwig Müller available to play for them?!

EURO '76

HOST COUNTRY: **YUGOSLAVIA**

RUNNERS-UP: **WEST GERMANY**

WINNERS: **CZECHOSLOVAKIA**

SCORE IN FINAL: **2 - 2**

(CZECHS WON 5-3 ON PENALTIES)

3rd PLACE: **HOLLAND**

4th PLACE: **YUGOSLAVIA**

NO. OF TEAMS ENTERED: **32**

NO. OF TEAMS IN FINAL: **4**

Now we're Euro-serious! Well, sort of...

England, Scotland, Northern Ireland and Wales took Euro '76 a bit more seriously than they had the previous tournaments. They decided they'd all like to win a group and get through to the second round. But there was a problem. If they insisted on being in the same group so that they could play the Home International Championship at the same time, then only one of them *could* get through!

So, for Euro '76, the four countries talked UEFA into putting them in separate groups. Did that mean England & Co. had suddenly realized the European

Championship was more important than their own competition? Not likely – they played the Home Internationals as well!

Killer Wales!

As it happened, only one of the four British countries reached the second round anyway. And it wasn't Scotland – who'd won the Home International Championship in 1976 – or England, who'd come second. It was little Wales.

What had made the difference? Maybe it was that, for the first time in their history, they'd got a full-time manager. What was his name? Something incredibly Welsh, like Jones or Evans? Davies or Llewellyn? No. It was Mike *Smith*, the most common name in England!

THESE ENGLISH ARE STRANGE PEOPLE, JONES

WHY'S THAT, JONES

MOST OF THEM ARE CALLED SMITH, JONES

We'll keep a welcome in the hillsides...

In the quarter-finals, Wales played Yugoslavia. They started badly, losing the first leg 2-0 and so needed to do something unforgettable when the Yugoslavs came to Wales for the return game.

Unfortunately Wales didn't (the Yugoslavs won 1-0) – but their fans did. After seeing their team miss a penalty and have two goals disallowed, beer cans were hurled on to the pitch and the Yugoslav goalkeeper was attacked. Maybe they should have remembered the words of their own famous song:

THERE'LL BE A WELCOME IN THE HILLSIDES
THERE'LL BE A WELCOME IN THE VALES
THIS LAND OF OURS WILL STILL BE SINGING
WHEN YOU COME HOME TO WALES!

SOME WELCOME!

THE MOST ORIGINAL WAY OF BUMPING UP THE CROWD AWARD...

Italy, who had their own football hooligans. To make sure there was no trouble when they played Poland in a Euro '76 group match the 90,000 crowd were joined by 4,000 riot police!

ENJOYING THE GAME?

Clubbing together!

It's well known that international teams find it difficult to build the same sort of team spirit as a club side. USSR came up with a clever way of solving this problem in their Euro '76 qualifying group – they twice picked the whole team from one club, Dynamo Kiev! What's more, they won both matches – 3-0 against Turkey and 2-0 against Eire.

Time out
The four countries who made it through to the final tournament were Yugoslavia (hosts), Czechoslovakia, Holland and West Germany. The results were:

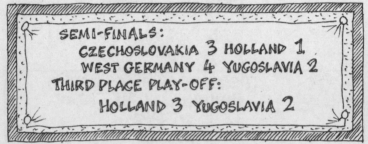

SEMI-FINALS:
CZECHOSLOVAKIA 3 HOLLAND 1
WEST GERMANY 4 YUGOSLAVIA 2
THIRD PLACE PLAY-OFF:
HOLLAND 3 YUGOSLAVIA 2

Question: What did these three games have in common?
Answer: They all went to extra time...
...and so did the final: Czechoslovakia versus West Germany.

After 90 minutes the score was 2-2. Into extra time they went, but after playing for a further 30 minutes the score was still 2-2. Now what?

It wasn't coin-tossing, as used in Euro '68. That had been tossed out. No, a new scheme was about to be used – for the first time in a major championship.

The penalty shoot-out!

Pay the penalty!
In case you've spent the past 25 years living in an

underground cave deep beneath an impenetrable jungle at the top of a high mountain – or anywhere else that neither TV, radio nor the paper boy/girl can reach, here's what happens with a penalty shoot-out:

FIVE DIFFERENT PLAYERS FROM EACH SIDE TAKE A PENALTY.

BOOT!

THE TEAM THAT SCORES THE MOST PENALTIES WINS THE MATCH.

IF SCORES ARE LEVEL AFTER ⑤ PENALTIES A "SUDDEN DEATH" STAGE FOLLOWS.

BANG!

NO, NOT THAT KIND OF "SUDDEN DEATH"! THIS ONE

PENALTIES ARE TAKEN IN TURN (BY DIFFERENT PLAYERS FROM THE FIRST FIVE)

(FIRST FIVE)

OOPS!

UNTIL ONE TEAM MISSES AND THE OTHER SCORES.

THERE ARE ALWAYS TWO RESULTS...

THE GOALKEEPING CHAMP OF THE WINNING TEAM. → TEARS OF JOY →

AND THE PENALTY-MISSING CHUMP WHOSE FAILURE MADE HIS TEAM LOSE →

I DIDN'T MISS ON PURPOSE!

JUST TEARS

65

*Penalty shoot-outs have nothing to do with football.
It's like shooting poor wee ducks at a fairground*

ALEX SMITH,
MANAGER OF
SCOTTISH
CLUB
ABERDEEN

The penalty shoot-out game

Here's your chance to experience the tension of the
penalty shoot-out! Find a friend – or, better still, a
bitter enemy! – and try the following five questions
about penalty shoot-outs. There are three answers
given to each question. Pick one answer each. Get
one of the two right answers and you score a GOAL!
Pick the wrong answer, though, and it's a MISS!

Penalty No. 1
The miss by Uli Hoeness in Euro '76 left
Czechoslovakia ahead by 4-3. Their player Panenka
duly scored his penalty to make it 5-3. What
happened?
a) Sepp Maier, the German goalie, dived the right way.
b) Panenka chipped his penalty softly over Maier's
diving body.
c) The ball went in off the bar.

Penalty No. 2

A penalty shoot-out decided the third-place team at the end of Euro '80. Which teams were involved?

a) Czechoslovakia.

b) West Germany.

c) Italy.

Penalty No. 3

In the Euro '96 semi-final between England and Germany, the scores were 5-5 when England's Gareth Southgate ran in to take the first sudden death penalty. Before then, what was Southgate's penalty-taking record?

a) He'd taken one penalty for his club, Aston Villa.

b) He'd taken one penalty for his previous club, Crystal Palace.

c) He'd never scored from a penalty in his whole career.

Penalty No. 4

The world record for a penalty shoot-out is currently held by two Argentine teams, Argentinos Juniors and Racing Club. Their contest in 1988 ended with the teams scoring how many penalties?

a) 21

b) 20

c) 19

Penalty No. 5

A penalty shoot-out with a difference was tried by the North American Soccer League which ran in the late 1970s. What was the difference? No penalties for a start – which is why it was just called a *shoot-out*. What happened?

a) A player dribbled towards the goal from 40 metres away.

b) He could shoot from anywhere he liked, and the opposing goalkeeper could come off his line.

c) He had to score within ten seconds.

Answers:

No. 1 It was one of the coolest penalties ever! **a)** GOAL! **b)** GOAL! **c)** MISS!

No. 2 a) GOAL! **b)** MISS! **c)** GOAL! What's more, the Czechs won again – this time, 9-8!

No. 3 a) MISS! **b)** GOAL! **c)** GOAL! Southgate had taken just one penalty in his career. It was for his previous club Crystal Palace, in the last minute of a match they were drawing 2-2. He missed it, hitting the post – and Palace were relegated that year!

No. 4 a) MISS! **b)** GOAL! **c)** GOAL! The score was 20-19 to Juniors.

No. 5 a) GOAL! **b)** GOAL! **c)** MISS! Players had only five seconds to score.

So, what's the score? Are you both still level? (If so, hopefully it's not at 0-0!) Then it's time for a question with only one right answer. It's a question of...

Sudden death!

The World Cup competition followed the European Championships in using penalty shoot-outs to

decide matches. In what year were they first used?
a) 1982
b) 1978

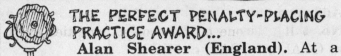

THE PERFECT PENALTY-PLACING PRACTICE AWARD...

Alan Shearer (England). At a training session the night before England's group match with Romania at Euro 2000, Shearer carefully took five practice penalties. He put each one in exactly the same place – suspecting that a spy from the Romanian camp would be watching and race straight back to tell their goalkeeper, Bogdan Stelea. Come the match and England were indeed awarded a penalty. Bogdan immediately bombed the way he's been told ... only to find sharp Shearer hitting his shot in the other direction! (Stelea smiled at the end, though. His team won the match 3-2 ... with an 88th minute penalty.)

Frightful Euro-fans

The terrible scenes during the Wales v. Yugoslavia match weren't the only occasions during Euro '76 when frightful Euro-freaks (sorry, "fans") have caused trouble...

● In the same year a linesman was hit by a missile thrown from the crowd after two Spanish players were sent off as Spain lost their qualifier against Yugoslavia 1-0.

● Frightful fans don't always go for the officials, though. A group of Greek fans travelled all the way to Budapest to see their country play Hungary in a Euro '88 qualifier only to be rewarded by a pathetic performance and a 3-0 defeat. Seriously annoyed at having wasted their time and money, the fans got their own back – by attacking their own players after the match!

WHY COULDN'T OUR TEAM RUN THIS FAST DURING THE MATCH?

THE MOST HOPELESS ATTEMPT AT CROWD CONTROL AWARD...
The Italian police. Attempting to quell fighting between spectators when England met Belgium in Turin during Euro '80, the Italian police fired tear gas into the crowd – only to have it blow back on to the pitch. The game had to be held up while the players recovered!

Neither is trouble outside the ground always caused by frightful fans; it can be the fault of pathetic players, too. After meeting Denmark in a Euro '76 qualifier, five Scots players were involved in a punch-up at a Copenhagen nightclub and banned for life from representing their country again. All this after Scotland had won the match 1-0!

HOST COUNTRY:
ITALY

RUNNERS-UP:
BELGIUM

3rd PLACE:
CZECHOSLOVAKIA

WINNERS:
WEST GERMANY
SCORE IN FINAL:
2 - 1

4th PLACE:
ITALY

NO. OF
TEAMS ENTERED:
32

NO. OF
TEAMS IN FINAL:
8

All change, part 1

Changes were made for Euro '80 which made it more like the competition we have today. Instead of a knockout tournament with just the four semi-finalists, Euro '80 had an eight-team final stage. Also, as now, the host country was chosen in advance – and given free entry into the last eight. Italy were the lucky team, so all they had to do was put their feet up while the other 31 countries fought it out.

Wait for it!

Euro '80 Group 1 made history. It included the

Republic of Ireland (Eire) and Northern Ireland, teams who had never played each other in an international match, even though these two parts of Ireland had been formed way back in 1921. So what did happen when the two finally met? It was a draw, without a goal being scored. What you might call the lack of the Irish!

You have been selected...

West Germany had little Malta in their group. Before the two teams met, Malta announced a squad of no less than 30 players. Was this because they had so many stars they couldn't decide who to put in their team? No – it was because most of their players were part-time, and they didn't know who'd be able to get off work! (Those that did wished they hadn't bothered: West Germany won 8-0.)

All change, part 2

West Germany went on to become Euro '80 champions, beating Belgium 2-1 in the final. And yet neither team had won their semi-finals!

How come?

Answer: There hadn't been any semi-finals! The eight teams in the final tournament had been put into two groups of four, each team playing the others in a mini-league. As the two top teams, West Germany and Belgium had gone straight into the final with the two second-placed teams playing for third and fourth positions.

Never again!

Those third-place play-off teams were host country Italy and Czechoslovakia. When they met, the Czechs won 9-8 on penalties. Exciting? No. The shoot-out had only come about after one of the dullest matches ever. How dull, exactly? Enough for UEFA to decide never to have a third-place match again!

THE BEST IMPERSONATION OF A YO-YO AWARD

Hans-Peter Breigel of Germany. After playing a storming first half in the final against Belgium, Breigel's second half timetable went:

46 mins: In a collision; leaves field for treatment...

49 mins: Back on again...

50 mins: Fouled, and injured again...

55 mins: Substituted!

90 mins: Comes back once more to collect winners medal.

Goalscoring feats and funny goals

There have been some great – and some grotty goals in Euro games. Can YOU score with these questions?

1 When Czechoslovakia played Holland during Euro '80 the game was stopped after an injury to a Dutch player. The referee then restarted the game with a dropped ball – except that he didn't bother to call a Czech player near: he just dropped it at the feet of the Holland player, Krol! Which team scored a goal immediately after?
a) Holland.
b) Czechoslovakia.

2 England didn't qualify for Euro '76 but a bit of goalscoring history was made when they beat Cyprus 5-0 in a group match. What was it?
a) England's goalkeeper scored a penalty.
b) One of the goals was scored direct from a corner.
c) All of the goals were scored by the same player.

3 In a Euro '92 game between France and Iceland, the French player Eric Cantona scored a weird and wonderful goal. Was it...
a) a header while he was on his hands and knees?
b) a bicycle kick from the edge of the penalty area?
c) a punch the referee didn't spot?

75

4 When Holland beat Yugoslavia 6-1 in a Euro 2000 quarter-final, their hero was striker Patrick Kluivert. He was credited with four goals ... with number three being really special. Why?

a) He didn't touch the ball.

b) He dribbled through straight from the kick-off.

c) He shot from inside his own half.

Answers: 1b) Krol was so surprised he gave the ball away and the Czechs raced off to open the scoring! **2c)** Malcolm Macdonald (an Englishman with a Scottish name, known as "SuperMac" to his fans) became the first player to score five goals in a Wembley international. **3a)** Perhaps he wanted to make the opposition grovel! **4a)** The goal was awarded to him after officials studied a video. Kluivert himself said, "I didn't think I'd touched it – but I'll take it!"

That is just a-mazing!

Euro 2000 saw one of the most entertaining goals ever scored in the Championships. It happened during the group game between Turkey and Germany, which ended in a shock 1-0 win to Turkey – and was the sort of goal that commentators dream about...

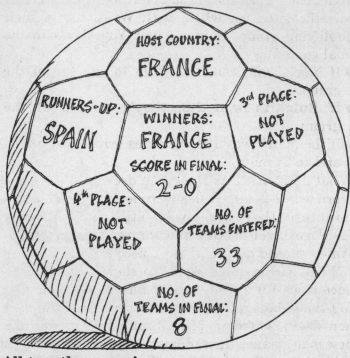

HOST COUNTRY:
FRANCE

RUNNERS-UP:
SPAIN

WINNERS:
FRANCE

3rd PLACE:
NOT PLAYED

SCORE IN FINAL:
2-0

4th PLACE:
NOT PLAYED

NO. OF TEAMS ENTERED:
33

NO. OF TEAMS IN FINAL:
8

All together, now!
England, Scotland, Wales and Northern Ireland were all equally successful in qualifying for the Euro '84 finals in France: none of them made it! Two out of the four came very close, though...

The bad luck of the Irish
Northern Ireland missed getting through by ten minutes! They would have been top of their group if West Germany hadn't beaten Albania in their last match – but they did, 2-1, scoring the winning goal just ten minutes from time.

The even worse luck of the Welsh

Wales came even closer than Northern Ireland. This was the situation when, with Wales top of their qualifying group, Bulgaria met Yugoslavia in the final game:

- If Yugoslavia won, they'd go to the top of the group.
- If Bulgaria won 2-0, they'd go top of the group.
- If the match was a draw, Wales would stay on top and go through.

What happened? As the game drew to a close the score was 2-2, and Wales were looking good. At 90 minutes, the score was still 2-2 ... only for Yugoslavia to score the winner in injury time! Wales missed out by ... er ... zero minutes!

What had inspired Wales to their best performance since Euro '76? It could have been their new full-time manager, who'd taken over from the very non-Welsh sounding Mike Smith. What was the new man's name, then? Something incredibly Welsh this time, like Jones or Evans or Davies or Llewellyn? No. It was the ex-Tottenham defender Mike *England*!

The luck of the Spanish, part 1

But the most sensational of the qualifying games had to be that between Malta and Spain. Going into the game, Spain were in second place to Holland and had scored fewer goals. In fact to overtake them, Spain needed not simply to win – but to score 11 goals more than Malta! This is what happened:

MALTA AREN'T HAPPY WHEN THEY START THE MATCH. TURNING UP AT THE STADIUM FOR A TRAINING SESSION THE EVENING BEFORE, THEY'D FOUND IT LOCKED UP AND THE LIGHTS OUT!

SPAIN ARE AWARDED A PENALTY - AND SENOR MISSES IT!

OOOPS!

DEGIORGIO OF MALTA IS BOOKED FOR TIME-WASTING WITH 80 MINUTES STILL TO GO!

MALTA FALTER. SPAIN SCORE TO LEAD 1-0.

MALTA EQUALIZE THROUGH DEGIORGIO! NOW SPAIN NEED TO WIN 12-1 TO GO ABOVE HOLLAND.

OOOPS!

AT HALF-TIME IT'S 3-1 TO SPAIN.

ONLY NINE MORE TO GO!

4-1 TO SPAIN, THE REFEREE IGNORES THE MOANS OF THE MALTESE GOALIE THAT SPANISH SUPPORTERS BEHIND THE GOAL HAD CHUCKED THINGS AT HIM.

THEY'D BETTER NOT THROW ANYTHING ELSE!

5-1 TO SPAIN.

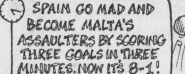

SPAIN GO MAD AND BECOME MALTA'S ASSAULTERS BY SCORING THREE GOALS IN THREE MINUTES. NOW IT'S 8-1!

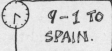 9 - 1 TO SPAIN.

 NOT LEARNING HIS LESSON, DEGIORGIO TRIES TIME-WASTING AGAIN AND TAKES AGES OVER A THROW-IN. THE REFEREE WAVES AWAY MALTESE PLEAS... AND SENDS HIM OFF!

 SPAIN SCORE AGAIN. NOW IT'S TEN MEN TO MALTA AND 10 - 1 TO SPAIN.

 11 - 1. NEARLY THERE! IF ONLY THEY HADN'T MISSED THAT PENALTY...

WE'D BE WINNING NOW IF IT WASN'T FOR YOU!

 SPAIN HIT THEIR 12th GOAL! AND IT'S SENOR THE PENALTY-MISSER WHO SCORES IT!

WE'RE WINNING NOW THANKS TO YOU!

 SPAIN HAVE WON 12 - 1. THEY'RE THROUGH TO THE FINALS AND A STUNNED (AND VERY SUSPICIOUS) HOLLAND ARE OUT!

I'M STUNNED!

I'M VERY SUSPICIOUS!

THE FULL MARKS FOR TRYING HARD FOR A HUNDRED YEARS WITHOUT MUCH SUCCESS AWARD...

Malta. As a British colony they've been part of the English FA since 1900 – giving them as long an official football history as Germany, and longer than Spain (who didn't have an FA until 1913), Brazil (1914) and France (1918)!

The luck of the Spanish, part 2

In the final tournament, Spain's luck continued to hold. The eight qualifiers were divided into two groups of four. This time semi-finals were being played, with the top team in each group meeting the runner-up in the other group.

Needing to beat West Germany to come top of their group Spain did so 1-0 ... with their goal coming in the last minute!

In the semi-final they met Denmark. No last-minute winners here, though. It was 1-1 after extra time ... but Spain won 5-4 on penalties!

The luck of the Spanish, part 3

In the Euro '84 final Spain met France, who'd had their own share of luck beating Portugal 3-2 in their semi-final after being 2-1 down. They'd won the game with their star player Michel Platini scoring in the last minute of extra time!

So somebody's luck had to run out – and it was Spain's. France became Euro '84 champions by winning the final 2-0 (with their second goal coming, yet again, in the last minute of the match!).

THE MOST HEARTLESS REFEREE AWARD...

Herr Roth, the German referee in charge of France v. Denmark, the opening game of the finals tournament. When Simonsen (Denmark) went down injured, the referee let play go on for a minute, even though the Danish player was waving his arms frantically for help. He had a broken leg.

Euro Star: Michel Platini

Fancy being a Euro Star and leading your country to a tremendous triumph? Here's a few tips on how to do it from Michel Platini, France's Euro '84 skipper.

1 LEARN HOW TO RECOGNIZE THE OPPOSITION'S GOAL:
In Euro '84 Platini...
- Scored in every game.
- Hit two hat-tricks.
- Bagged nine of France's 15 goals!

OOH! OOH! LOOK! THE OPPOSITION'S GOAL!

2 GIVE YOURSELF A GOOD START IN LIFE... CHOOSE YOUR DAD CAREFULLY:
- Marvellous Michel's Dad was a football coach.

I'LL TAKE THE ONE IN THE MIDDLE!

3 DON'T WASTE YOUR TEENAGE YEARS WORRYING ABOUT GIRLS:
- It's true that, when he was a teenager, Platini was mad about Nancy. But his Nancy wasn't the name of a girlfriend, it was the name of the French football league club he made his debut for when he was just 17!

NO, I WON'T BE A GOAL-POST!

④ GET A TASTE FOR ITALIAN FOOD:
● Platini played for Juventus and was the Italian league's top scorer three times.

⑤ INVENT THE CURLING FREE-KICK 15 YEARS BEFORE DAVID BECKHAM:
● It was Michel Platini's speciality and he scored loads of goals with it - including France's first goal against Spain in the Euro '84 final.

⑥ LEARN TO COUNT UP TO THREE:
He was voted European Footballer of the Year in 1983... and 1984... and again in 1985!

⑦ DON'T THINK THAT JUST BECAUSE YOU WERE A STAR PLAYER YOU'LL BE A STAR COACH:
● After he'd finished playing, Michel Platini became France's coach. With him in charge they qualified for the Euro '92 finals - but did badly. He resigned.

⑧ BUT YOU CAN ALWAYS BE A STAR SUPPORTER!
● When the World Cup was played in France in 1998, Michel the Magnifique was there to see every game his country played. Mind you, he did get in for free. He was one of the main organizers!

HOT-DOG, PLEASE!

EURO '88

HOST COUNTRY:
WEST GERMANY

RUNNERS-UP:
USSR

WINNERS:
HOLLAND
SCORE IN FINAL:
2-0

3rd PLACE:
NOT PLAYED

4th PLACE:
NOT PLAYED

NO. OF TEAMS ENTERED:
33

NO. OF TEAMS IN FINAL:
8

Double Dutch

Euro '88 was Holland's competition from start to finish. In their qualifying group, striker Johnny Bosman completed an amazing feat during the match against Cyprus. He scored seven goals – even though Holland only won 4-0!

How did he do it?

Answer: With some help from the more horrendous Holland fans. After Bosman had scored in the first minute they started celebrating by throwing smoke bombs. One of them hit and injured the Cypriot goalkeeper, Charitou, who had to be carried off. The game continued, with Bosman scoring four goals in an 8-0 win, but then Cyprus appealed to UEFA that they'd been cheated.

I THOUGHT CHARITOU BEGAN AT HOME!

UEFA promptly awarded the game to Cyprus – only for Holland to appeal, claiming that they couldn't be blamed for their stupid smoke-bombing fans and that if the game was given to Cyprus then *they* would be cheated!

So UEFA changed their mind again, and decided that the match should be replayed. It was, and Bosman scored another three goals as Holland won by the official result of 4-0!

Three lions, three defeats!

In the finals in West Germany, Holland were drawn in the same group as England. England had qualified brilliantly, scoring 19 goals and only giving away one – but in the finals they were useless, losing all three of their games.

Against Holland they lost 3-1, with all of the Dutch goals being scored by their star striker Marco Van Basten. England's defenders obviously failed to Marco him tightly enough!

Are you blind, ref?

In the semi-final, Holland played their old rivals West Germany and won 2-1. It was a controversial match, with the referee awarding a disputed penalty to each team.

Spectators are always telling referees to get their eyes tested, but in this case it might have been good advice. Before the match, the ref (and his linesmen) had been sent plane tickets and had cheerfully used them – not noticing that they were for travel to the German city of Stuttgart when the match was being played 300 miles away in Hamburg!

> **NO EXCUSES, YOUR NAME'S GOING IN THE BOOK!**

> **ER.. REF, THE GAME'S OVER HERE!**

Marvellous Marco

Holland went on to become Euro '88 champions by beating USSR 2-0 in the final and once again it was marvellous Marco Van Basten who was their hero, scoring the goal of the tournament. Try it for yourself on your school pitch:

POSITION YOURSELF ON THE RIGHT SIDE OF THE PENALTY AREA, ABOUT A METRE FROM THE GOAL LINE.

GOAL

YOU

NOW GET A FRIEND TO HIT THE BALL ACROSS TO YOU FROM THE LEFT WING.

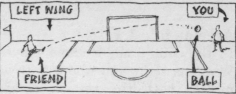

IF IT COMES OVER ON THE GROUND, MAKE HIM DO IT AGAIN. IT'S GOT TO BE IN THE AIR.

WHEN THE BALL ARRIVES, DON'T LET IT BOUNCE; YOU'VE GOT TO WHACK IT WITH YOUR RIGHT FOOT "ON THE VOLLEY" - THAT IS BEFORE IT BOUNCES...

AND HIT IT JUST INSIDE THE POST ON THE SIDE OF THE GOAL... FURTHEST AWAY FROM YOU!

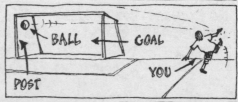

AFTER YOU'VE TRIED AND FAILED A THOUSAND TIMES YOU'LL REALIZE WHY VAN BASTEN'S GOAL IS USUALLY DESCRIBED AS "IMPOSSIBLE"!

Many would say that this game was one of the best that Marvellous Marco ever played. Not so long after he began to suffer with the bad ankle which eventually forced him to retire from the game. He'd been one of the most graceful players ever – as the doctor who looked after him pointed out:

Marco played football like a ballerina, but eventually his ankle couldn't stand the strain

Euro Star: Ruud Gullit

Of all the stars in Holland's 1988
team, their captain Ruud Gullit
was the one who stood out above
all others – and not just because
of his immediately recognizable
dreadlocks!

Gullit had the ability to play
in any position on the pitch. He began his
career as a sweeper with the Dutch club Haarlem,
then moved to midfield with another Dutch club
PSV Eindhoven, and finally ended up as a striker
with the top Italian team AC Milan.

He was certainly seen as one of Holland's most
important players during Euro '88. Before the final
against their team, German journalists kept ringing
his hotel room during the night trying to stop him
getting enough sleep!

ARE YOU
SLEEPING OK,
MR GULLIT?

As a player Ruud Gullit was known all over the world – except by passport checkers at airports. Why? Because the name in his passport isn't Ruud Gullit at all. It's Rudi Dil, the name he was always known by as a child: "Rudi" the nickname, and "Dil", his mother's surname.

Rampaging Ruud was always very grown up for his age. Holland have a National Youth Team for different age groups – and Gullit was big enough (and good enough) to play for the 16–18s when he was only 15!

Mind you, he hardly ever looked his age. He was only 16 years old when he grew his first moustache!

He was big and strong, too, with a powerful shot. In schoolboy football he'd always want to take any free kicks his team won – and use his top tactic. Here's what he did:

Waited untill the opposing team had put their players into a wall.

and thumped the ball as hard as he could at one of the kids in the wall! If the kid jumped out of the way then Ruud would usually score goal! If the kid didn't jump out of the way he got hurt by the ball - and boy did he bawl! That way, the next time his team got a free kick, the kid's mum would yell from the touch line and Ruud would have

stay away from that big boy!

less of a wall to deal with...while the kids who were still in it, shaking like jellies, would make sure they jumped out of the way!

Jelly legs

In his later career, of course, he had to change the trick. When he discovered that most of the defenders he came up against when he was playing for AC Milan didn't have their mums in the crowd telling them to duck, Ruud practised bending the ball round cardboard cut-outs instead.

THIS OTHER TEAM ISN'T PUTTING UP MUCH OF A FIGHT!

His best childhood friend was a boy he met when he was ten years old and waiting to catch a tram. The boy's name was Frank Rijkaard, and after they'd met they would spend hours playing football together.

Much later, when Ruud had become a major star and was transferred from PSV Eindhoven to AC Milan for a then world record of £6 million, who else was playing in the team? Frank Rijkaard!

And when Ruud lifted the Henri Delaunay trophy as captain of the Euro '88 champions, who was there with him collecting his own winner's medal? You've guessed it – Frank Rijkaard!

Ruud Gullit received many honours in his playing career, winning the European Cup with AC Milan and being named European Footballer of the Year in 1987. Then, when he turned his hand to coaching, he became the first foreign coach in English football to lead a side to a trophy when his team Chelsea won the FA Cup in 1997.

But Ruud Gullit's proudest honour is probably the oddest-named. In recognition of his part in Holland's Euro '88 triumph, he was made a "Knight of the Queen (of Holland)".

Yes, for Ruud Gullit the Euro '88 final was definitely a great day followed by a good knight!

Euro Battles 2: Germany v. Holland

Holland and Germany are the England and Scotland of the continent; when the two countries play each other at football, sparks fly!

Is it a case of Horrible Holland or Grisly Germany? Find out with these five foul questions...

1 When Holland beat West Germany in the Euro '88 semi-final, it was their first victory over them in 32 years. In the Leidseplein Square in Amsterdam, the Dutch fans went wild. They sang and they danced – and they threw things in the air. What sort of things?

a) Bicycles.

b) Hats.

c) Each other.

2 The players in that Euro '88 game weren't terribly friendly with each other; the only two who swapped shirts after the match were Ronald Koeman of Holland and Olaf Thon of Germany. But that didn't mean they were pals.

What did Koeman say he did with Thon's shirt afterwards?

a) Used it to light the fire.

b) Used it as a door mat.

c) Used it as a sheet of paper.

3 One of West Germany's finest wins, and Holland's saddest defeats, was the 1974 World Cup final. West Germany won 2-1 after Holland had taken a first-minute lead. It was said afterwards that the Dutch had been over-confident. True or false?

4 Holland and (a combined) Germany both qualified for Euro '92, only to find themselves in the same group. What did the Dutch fans do while the German national anthem was being played before their match?

a) Sang a rude song.

b) Let off stink bombs.

c) Whistled.

5 Holland won that Euro '92 game 3-1. With only a few minutes to go, the Dutch players were enjoying themselves so much they all refused to come off, so their manager couldn't bring on a substitute when he wanted to. True or false?

6 The teams also met in a nasty World Cup '90 second-round match, won 2-1 by West Germany. In this game Holland's star defender Frank Rijkaard was sent off for something he did to the German striker Rudi Voller. What was it?

a) Bit his ear.

b) Gave him a mouthful.

c) Punched his nose.

Answers: 1a) What's more, they were shouting things like: "Hooray, we've got our bikes back!" Why? Because they had long memories. When Germany had occupied Holland during the Second World War they'd locked away everybody's bicycles.
2c) A sheet of toilet paper to be exact; he wiped his bum on it. What you might call enemies to the bitter end!
3 True. The Dutch team admitted they wanted to humiliate the Germans so they concentrated on passing the ball around instead of on trying to score more goals.
4c) They whistled so loudly they drowned the music and the German players ran off for a kick-about while their own anthem was still playing!

Afterwards Holland's fans had even more to whistle about: they won the game 3-1. **5** False. Only the senior players wouldn't come off, so the manager had to pick on one of the junior players – a young Dennis Bergkamp. To soften the blow (Bergkamp had just scored Holland's third goal) the unhappy player was told, "Dennis, we're giving the fans the chance to clap you." **6b)** Rijkaard claimed that Voller had said something rude to him, so he gave him a mouthful back. The difference was that Rijkaard's mouthful wasn't of words – but of spit!

THE TEAM MOST LIKELY TO SWAP SHIRTS WITH THEIR OPPONENTS AWARD...

Holland, during Euro '96. After the controversies of 1988, Holland came prepared. In their kit bag were no less than 550 shirts – plus 900 pairs of shorts and 500 pairs of socks! Were all these strips worn? If so, one item was in short supply. The players would have had to use their underpants more than once because they'd only brought 140 pairs of them. Phwor!

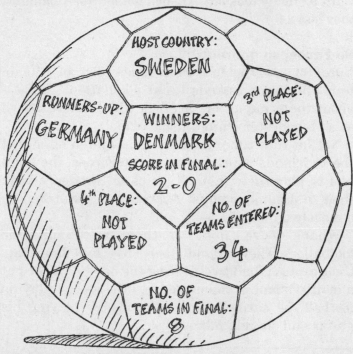

HOST COUNTRY: SWEDEN

RUNNERS-UP: GERMANY

WINNERS: DENMARK

3rd PLACE: NOT PLAYED

SCORE IN FINAL: 2-0

4th PLACE: NOT PLAYED

NO. OF TEAMS ENTERED: 34

NO. OF TEAMS IN FINAL: 8

Anything to declare?

With the largest number of entries so far, Euro '92 actually began in May 1990 – but only just. The first

IT'S THE EURO TROPHY YOU'RE AIMING TO LIFT, NOTHING ELSE!

game, Iceland v. Albania, nearly didn't happen. Some of the Albanian players were arrested on suspicion of shoplifting when their flight stopped for a while at London Airport. Eventually

97

they were allowed to continue their journey – and
Euro '92 really took off! (Though not for the Albanians;
they lost 2-0.)

So Faroe, so good-oh!

Euro '92 saw the first-ever appearance of a team
from the Faroe Islands (total population 47,000 –
about the same as the average Old Trafford crowd
at a Manchester United home game!).

Not (at that time) having a grass pitch on any of
the 18 islands which make up the Faroes, the team
had to play their "home" games in Sweden – with
their first game, against Austria, being watched by
a measly crowd of 1,544.

What's more, none of them were full-time
footballers. They all had other jobs – and Jakoksen,
their captain, had two! During the day he worked at
a dentist's and in the evenings, if he wasn't playing
football, he earned some extra money playing his
guitar and singing folk songs!

The Faroes' opening game was against once-mighty Austria. Not surprisingly, the Faroes weren't confident. As skipper Jakoksen prophesied,

We know we will suffer some heavy defeats, but we are proud to represent our country

Furious Euro's question
Was Jakoksen right or wrong?
Answer: Right *and* wrong. Amongst their eight qualifying games the Faroes suffered a 7-0 defeat against Yugoslavia and a 5-0 defeat to Northern Ireland. But in that first match they caused the biggest Euro-shock ever, beating Austria 1-0!

Can somebody hold my paintbrush?
Yugoslavia won the Faroes' group, with Denmark in the runners-up position. So off to Sweden went Yugoslavia for the finals ... leaving behind a civil war, with different parts of the country (Serbia, Bosnia and Croatia) doing some very nasty things to each other – Bosnia in particular.

In an attempt to make them all stop – and make them see that the rest of the world disapproved of the war – the world's politicians "imposed sanctions" against Yugoslavia. This is a bit like when your teacher takes your ball away to stop you fighting in the playground. And, in the case of the Yugoslavian footballers, that's exactly what *did* happen. As part of the sanctions, their team was thrown out of Euro

'92 and their place taken by group runners-up Denmark.

This decision may have come as a shock to Yugoslavia, but it came as an even bigger shock to Denmark, who only heard about it ten days before the finals began! Half their players were on holiday and their manager, Richard Moller Neilsen, had just started decorating his kitchen!

Taylor's team stitched up!
Denmark were drawn in the same finals group as England – who had just managed to qualify ahead of Eire and Poland – and the game between them ended in a 0-0 draw.

England followed up the Denmark draw with another, 0-0 against France, to find themselves having to beat Sweden to stay in the competition. They didn't, so they didn't. After being 1-0 up at half-time, they lost 2-1 and Sweden and Denmark went through to the semi-finals from their group.

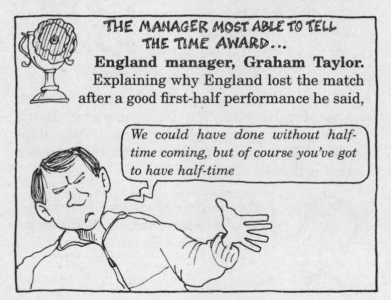

THE MOST GEOGRAPHICALLY CONFUSED MANAGER AWARD...

England manager, Graham Taylor, *again!* He said about Sweden,

> *They came at us playing direct football. They were more English than the English*

> I SAY, OLD CHAP, MIND AWFULLY IF I PASS ?

Some you lose, some you win!

Sweden then lost to Germany 3-2, while Denmark had to play Holland. The Dutch manager, Rinus Michels, was so sure of getting through to a final against fellow group members and bitter rivals Germany that he prophesied,

> *I've always said we'll meet Germany twice in this tournament. Next time it will be difficult again*

He was wrong. There wasn't a next time – Denmark beat Holland 5-3 on penalties after the match had ended 2-2.

And who missed the crucial penalty for Holland? None other than their Euro '88 star, Marco Van Basten. Talk about a black Marc!

THE LONGEST MEMORY AWARD...
Mort Olsen, Denmark's captain who, after Denmark had won the semi-final penalty shoot-out said, *"Luck evens itself out in the end."* He was talking about the fact that Denmark had lost a semi-final shoot-out before ... eight years before, in Euro '84!

MORT NEVER FORGETS

Great Danes

The story ended with Denmark, the country who'd only stepped in after Yugoslavia had been banned, beating Germany 2-0 in the final to become Euro '92 champions. Not bad for a team who'd been knocked out in the qualifying round!

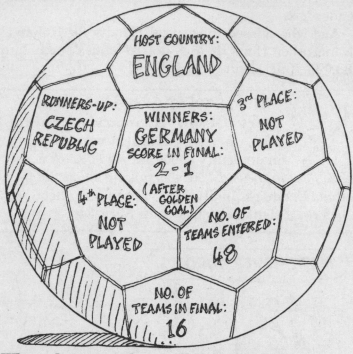

EURO '96

HOST COUNTRY: **ENGLAND**

RUNNERS-UP: **CZECH REPUBLIC**

3rd PLACE: **NOT PLAYED**

WINNERS: **GERMANY** SCORE IN FINAL: **2 - 1** (AFTER GOLDEN GOAL)

4th PLACE: **NOT PLAYED**

NO. OF TEAMS ENTERED: **48**

NO. OF TEAMS IN FINAL: **16**

Where have you been all this time?

Question: The largest ever number of countries – 48 – entered for Euro '96. Why hadn't they done so before?

Answer: Because most of them didn't exist. Countries like Moldova and Georgia had previously been part of the USSR; the break-up of Yugoslavia into several smaller countries led to the arrival of teams from the likes of Croatia, Macedonia and the commentator's nightmare Bosnia-Herzegovina; Czechoslovakia had split into the Czech Republic and Slovakia.

IT'S GREAT FOR WHEN THE WEATHER GETS COLD!

BOSNIA-HERZEGOVINA

This huge number of new entries gave UEFA a problem. If they left the number of places in the finals at eight it would mean that, because European teams had 13 guaranteed places in the World Cup finals, it would be harder for them to qualify for their own championships than it was for the world tournament! Solution: for Euro '96, UEFA increased the number of places in the finals to 16.

THE CHEAPEST TRAVEL TO AWAY GAMES AWARD...

San Marino's part-time goalkeeper, Benedittioni. As he was a travel agent by trade, not only did he play for his country he also drove their team coach!

WHERE'S BENEDITTIONI?

HE WENT TO WARM UP THE BUS...

Easy!

England had no difficulty at all in reaching the last 16. They didn't lose a single qualifying game – mainly because they didn't have to play any! As host country for Euro '96 they went straight into the finals.

Of the other British countries, Wales and Northern Ireland didn't get close to qualifying. Scotland, though, made it for the second championships in a row.

Question: Who did they get in their finals group?
Answer: Switzerland, Holland ... and England!

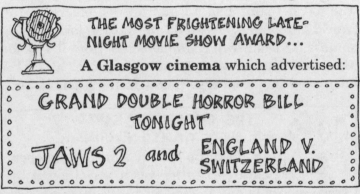

THE MOST FRIGHTENING LATE-NIGHT MOVIE SHOW AWARD...

A Glasgow cinema which advertised:

GRAND DOUBLE HORROR BILL TONIGHT

JAWS 2 and ENGLAND V. SWITZERLAND

THAT WAS TERRIFYING!

I TOLD YOU WE SHOULD HAVE SEEN JAWS 2!

Agh! Not you again!

And it was England who were to blame for Scotland being knocked out – not once, but twice!

1 When the two teams met at Wembley, England won 2-0.

2 Then, in the final matches of the group, England raced into a 4-0 lead against Holland. If the score had stayed like that, Scotland would have gone through to the next round because of their better goal difference. But it didn't stay like that. With just 13 minutes of the match left, England let in a goal. It was enough to give Holland the better goals record – and Scotland went out. Did the English do it on purpose? No, of course they didn't ... but try telling that to a Scot! As one fan said:

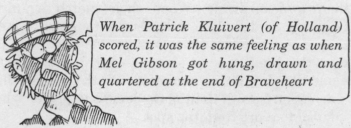

> *When Patrick Kluivert (of Holland) scored, it was the same feeling as when Mel Gibson got hung, drawn and quartered at the end of Braveheart*

THE ACCIDENTAL SUPER-SUB AWARD...

Alfonso Perez of Spain, who came on in the group match against Bulgaria with his team ready to take a free kick, and positioned himself in the middle of the Bulgarian wall. The kick was taken, only to hit Alfonso the Accident-prone, and shoot into the net! He'd unintentionally scored with his very first touch!

The pain in Spain

In the quarter-finals England came up against

Spain. It just wasn't Spain's day. They...

- had two goals disallowed for offside (one of which wasn't offside)...
- had two penalty claims turned down...
- then, after the match ended in a 0-0 draw, they lost the penalty shoot-out with England keeper David Seaman saving two of their penalties.

In other words, after a no g-olé! draw they were beaten by England's top g-olé!

England pay the penalty
In the semi-final, though, England got a taste of their own medicine. When their match against Germany ended 1-1 and went into extra time, they...

- hit the post...
- and then lost 6-5 on penalties with the Aston Villa defender Gareth Southgate being the player who failed to score from the spot.

Haven't I seen you somewhere before?

The other semi-final, between the Czech Republic and France, also went to a penalty shoot-out. The Czechs won it 6-5, but nearly got themselves disqualified in the process! After the two sides had both scored their first five penalties, France missed their sixth. Up stepped Lubos Kubik for the Czechs to try and win the game – only to be sent away by the referee.

Why?

Answer: He'd already taken the first of the five penalties and thought it was a case of going round again! But the rule is that every player in the team must take one before that happens. So the Czech captain, Miroslav Kadlec had to do the job – and scored, to put his team into the final.

Goalden goals!

Germany v. the Czech Republic was a game with a difference. It was decided *without* a penalty shoot-out! That's not to say one of the teams was ahead after 90 minutes, though. The score at full time was 1-1. But only four minutes of extra time were played.

Why?

Answer: Under the new "golden goal" rule brought in for the tournament, if a team scored during extra time that was it – the match ended instantly. So when Germany scored after four minutes the referee blew for the goal and full time together. Germany were Euro '96 champions!

THE WORST-EDUCATED INTERNATIONAL SALES FORCE AWARD...
The Sweatshirt Company whose advert went a bit wrong and came out as offering supporters Euro '96 Swear-shirts!

Stamped out!

If England had gone on to win Euro '96 the Royal Mail planned to issue a special set of five first-class stamps featuring a star player...

- holding the Euro Championship Cup aloft after England win the final.

- scoring the winner in the penalty shoot-out against Germany.
- playing in the quarter-final against Spain.
- scoring a goal in the opening match against Switzerland.
- being called up for the England squad – at the age of 42!

Furious Euro's question
Who was the player?

Answer: Comic book hero Roy of the Rovers. It couldn't have been a real member of the England squad because no living person is allowed to feature on a British stamp other than a member of the Royal Family – not even Michael Owen. But as Gareth Southgate didn't score his penalty, England didn't reach the final and win so the whole issue was scrapped – at a cost of £50,000!

Euro Battles 3: England v. Germany

England's semi-final against Germany during Euro '96 was just the latest in a whole series of battles between the two sides. And sometimes there have been battles off the field as well. Here's a blow-by-blow account...

1914 England international Steve Bloomer retires from the game and goes to coach ... in Germany! He's welcomed with open arms. The trouble is, they're firearms – Germany and Britain have just kicked off the First World War. Bloomer is locked up until 1918. When he gets out, does he run for it? No, he carries on coaching! Blooming amazing.

1938 England play Germany in Berlin – and there's controversy before the match even begins. Should the team give the straight-arm Nazi salute during the German national anthem? The players don't want to, but the British Ambassador, Sir Nevile Henderson, thinks they should in case Germany's leader Adolf

Hitler is offended. So the team salute – then whack Adolf's team 6-3. (Which probably offended him even more: 15 months later Germany and Britain were at war again!)

1954 West Germany, the reigning world champions after beating Hungary in the 1954 World Cup Final, travel to Wembley – and England beat them 3-1. Their third goal is a super chip from England star Len Shackleton ... a player who is straight-talking as well as straight-shooting. He later writes an autobiography which includes a chapter entitled *"What the average [football club] director knows about football"* ... and leaves the page blank!

1956 Another 3-1 victory for England, this time in West Germany. The highlight is a goal by the

19-year-old Manchester United star Duncan Edwards who beats player after player before smacking in one of the hardest shots the 100,000 crowd has ever seen. For the rest of the game they're calling him "Boom-Boom" Edwards!

1966 England v. West Germany. The old enemies meet again at Wembley.

Furious Euro's question
What was the score?
Answer: 1-0 to England! No, not 4-2. That was the World Cup final in July, the most famous England v. West Germany match of all time, won by England, with their much-disputed third goal being awarded only after the referee consulted his flag-waving linesman.

But in a clever bit of spying, England had also played the West Germans at Wembley in February that year. The game should have given the Germans a warning: England won 1-0 ... with West Germany having a goal disallowed after the referee consulted his flag-waving linesman!

**THE MOST INTELLIGENT THING
EVER SAID BY AN ENGLAND
MANAGER ABOUT ENGLAND FANS
AWARD...**

Alf Ramsey after England's 1-0 win in February was booed by the Wembley crowd:

Listen to them moan! But those people will be going mad if we beat West Germany by a goal in the World Cup final

1968 Off-the-field trickery in Germany. Before a friendly held in Hanover (the one which took place four days before England played Yugoslavia in the Euro '68 semi-final) representatives of the big German sports companies Puma and Adidas approach the England players and offer them money to wear their boots in the match. Some players grab the money, wear the boots (something guaranteed to give you sore feet) – and England lose 1-0 to go down to their first ever defeat against Germany.

1970 On-the-field trickery in Mexico when the two teams meet in the World Cup quarter-final. England are 2-0 ahead only for Germany to pull back and win 3-2 in extra time.

1972 The Euro '72 second-round tie. After being

114

outplayed at Wembley and fortunate only to lose 3-1, England travel to Germany determined to get a few more kicks this time. They manage it – by kicking the Germans instead of the ball! The game ends in a 0-0 draw, but England give away 27 free kicks. Germany's manager, Helmut Schoen, describes England's tackling as *"Brutal!"*

1975 A double celebration for England. It's their 100th international at Wembley and, by winning 2-0, they become the first team to beat the West Germans since they won the 1974 World Cup.

1978 A German home win, by 2-1, after England had been ahead. The man who makes the difference by scoring the German equalizer is their substitute Ronnie Worm (who must have glowed with pleasure – making him a glow-Worm!).

1982 Another meeting, this time in a second-round group match in the World Cup. The game ended in a 0-0 draw, and here is the most exciting part of the commentary:

And the referee blows his whistle for full time

1985 The rarest of England v. Germany rarities! The teams meet in a friendly played in Mexico City as part of a mini-tournament – and a German misses a penalty! England goalkeeper Peter Shilton saves a spot-kick from Andreas Brehme and England win 3-0.

1987 Germany win a friendly 3-1, but Neil Webb doesn't care. Running on as substitute for a certain England-manager-to-be-but-not-for-very-long Glenn Hoddle, Webb becomes the 1000th player to represent England.

1990 West Germany go ahead in World Cup wins between the two countries. Their semi-final match finishes 1-1 after extra time … only for the Germans to win the penalty shoot-out 4-3! Chris Waddle and Stuart Pearce were the unfortunates who missed for England. Chris Waddle said of that terrible moment:

> *When I missed it, I went and kicked the post. Then I crouched down for a bit. But the one thing I thought was, I'm not going to cry on the pitch. Then when I got down to the training room, there were about seven or eight of the team crying. I got changed and put a towel over my head and cried into the towel*

1993 Another friendly, this time in Detroit, USA as part of a four-team mini-tournament with the USA and Brazil designed to drum up interest in the non-American kind of football before the World Cup was held there in 1994. Germany win 2-1 ... but the most interesting thing about the game is that although played on grass, the pitch is indoors!

1996 And so to Euro '96. Another semi-final, another penalty shoot-out – and another German win after Gareth Southgate's blunder. England manager Terry Venables says exactly what he thinks of Germany when he's asked a question at a press conference:

2000 Just like the buses. You don't play against each other for a while, then two games come along together! First England and Germany are drawn in the same group at Euro 2000, and England win their group match 1-0 with a goal from Alan Shearer. Then, just four months later, they're at it again. This time it's a 2002 World Cup qualifiying match – and they've been drawn in the same group! To add to the occasion it's the last game ever at the old Wembley Stadium before it's knocked down to make way for a new one. So what happens?

a) England celebrate with a win.

b) It's a friendly draw.

c) Germany win and spoil the party.

> **Answer: c)** Old friends only party after the game. Germany win 1-0.

HOST COUNTRY:
BELGIUM
and
HOLLAND

RUNNERS-UP:
ITALY

WINNERS:
FRANCE
SCORE IN FINAL:
2 - 1
(AFTER GOLDEN GOAL)

NO. OF TEAMS ENTERED:
51

NO. OF TEAMS IN FINAL:
16

It's the big one!

Euro 2000, for the first time in the history of the European Championships, was jointly hosted by two countries: Belgium and Holland. They both got a free place in the finals which meant that, with a huge 51 countries entering, it was harder than ever to qualify...

Training on porridge

Wales tried a new approach. Instead of staying at a luxurious hotel for their training sessions, manager Bobby Gould gave his players a spell in prison! He took them to stay at Prescoed Open Prison, arguing that – apart from being able to use the prison's terrific facilities – it showed the players how lucky they were to be playing for their country (and presumably to encourage them to play with more conviction!).

Sadly, it didn't work. Wales's defence regularly failed to lock out the opposition and they finished well down in their group. Gould may have picked up some tips on escaping, though: after Wales lost 4-0 to Italy he resigned!

HE'S GONE!

Bombs away!

England had manager problems too, with new man Kevin Keegan taking over half-way through their campaign. Immediately he inspired midfield player Paul Scholes to bang in a Wembley hat trick as England beat Poland 3-0. What you might call a score of three Scholes to nil!

Carried away by this, Keegan told Scholes that his job in their next match against Sweden was to "drop hand grenades all over the pitch" – meaning "pop up everywhere and cause problems". Unfortunately the Manchester United star got the wrong end of the stick. He simply bombed about, committed two bad fouls and got sent off, leaving England to struggle to a 0-0 draw.

Scotland

Scottish defender Matt Elliott also got sent off, in Scotland's 1-1 draw away to the Faroe Islands. Why and how? Just before half-time he slapped the Faroese defender Todi Jonsson round the face and a French woman who saw it happen reported him to the referee!

Furious Euro's question: What was she doing on the pitch?
Answer: Her name was Madame Nelly Viennot – and she was one of the referee's linesmen! (Well, lineswoman in her case.)

For the Faroe Islands to get a draw was only fair-o. In Scotland they'd been beaten 2-1, with the first goal against them being hotly disputed. Here's why:

THE BALL WENT OUT OF PLAY.

BALL 1

TO HURRY THINGS UP, PLAY WAS RESTARTED WITH ANOTHER BALL...

BALL 2

WHILE SOMEBODY WENT AFTER BALL NO.1,

PICKED IT UP...

BALL 1

AND THREW IT BACK ON THE PITCH,

BALL 1

BALL 1 BACK ON THE PITCH

NOT REALIZING BALL NO.2 WAS NOW IN PLAY! SECONDS LATER, WITH SOME OF THE FAROESE DEFENDERS CONCENTRATING ON BALL NO.1...

BALL 1

CRAIG BURLEY WHACKED BALL NO.2 IN THE NET!

BALL 2

I'M SEEING DOUBLE!

Just wait till I grow up!

Other little countries had qualifying games to remember. On 14 October 1998, Liechtenstein gained their first ever Euro-victory, just hanging on for a 2-1 win over Azerbaijan. Their hero, goal-keeper Peter Jehle, was also a first-timer. He was making his début. Mind you, if he'd made it much earlier he'd have been wearing a nappy: Jehle was just 16 years old.

Leboeuf le bouche!
Tiny Andorra did well, too. Before their game against world champions France, the French defender Frank Leboeuf (in English, Frank The-beef) opened his big bouche and beefed:

I'm not here to play against Andorra. I'm not here to play against second-class teams

What happened? France just scraped a 1-0 victory with a penalty six minutes from the end. Who had to be there to score the penalty? Frank "sometimes I talk a lot of bull" Leboeuf!

Off-play in the play-offs
With two hosts and nine automatic qualifiers, the remaining four places in the Euro 2000 finals were decided by play-off matches. In one of these, the Republic of Ireland met Turkey. They were tough games, but even tougher afterwards! At the end of the match in Turkey, one home fan celebrated by punching Ireland's Tony Cascarino, and riot police

were needed to clear the pitch. His manager, Mick McCarthy, said:

> *I expect my players to battle on the field, but I don't expect them to have to fight their way off it!*

Unhappy Hosts 1

When the finals got underway, joint-host country Belgium proved to have a team which melted as quickly as the chocolate their country is famous for. It didn't help having a hot-head named Filip for a goalkeeper. Belgium had beaten Sweden 2-1 in their first game but flapper Filip had given the Swedes their goal by treading on the ball instead of kicking it. Then, with Belgium needing to beat Turkey to stay in the competition, foul Filip got sent off for racing out of his penalty area and flattening a Turkish forward. He apologized to his team-mates afterwards, but really they might have seen it coming as their crazy keeper's full name was Filip ... de Wilde!

THE TOO HOT-HEADED FOR SAFETY AWARD...

No, not Filip de Wilde but **Spain's five chefs**. Brought along to cook paella for the squad, they were shown the red card by the Dutch fire brigade. They'd planned to cook in tents but were told this was too dangerous and were sent off to do their work in proper indoor kitchens.

Unhappy Hosts 2

The other joint-hosts, Holland, fared rather better. They won every game in their group, then sailed into the semi-finals with a 6-1 win against Yugoslavia. There they met Italy and...

– missed a penalty in the first half

– missed another penalty in the second half

– then, after the match had finished 0-0, they missed another three penalties during the shoot-out.

Result: Italy went through to the final – and, for missing all those chances, Holland paid the penalty!

Unhappy Hosts 3

Portugal had started well, winning their group and helping to knock England and Germany out. They too made the semi-finals, where they played France. There, claimed Portugal, they were robbed. They lost 2-1 to France, the winner coming from a disputed penalty. In a furious scuffle three of Portugal's players surrounded the referee, Gunter Benko. Striker Nuno Gomes pushed him in the chest, team-mate and defender Abel Xavier grabbed him by the arm and midfielder Paulo Bento tried to grab the referee's – what?

a) Pencil.

b) Red card.

c) Whistle.

Answer: b) To stop him showing it to Gomes! After an enquiry, the three players were banned for between six and nine months. Were Portugal sorry? No. They suggested their defeat had all been a nasty plan, saying, "We are a little country with little influence. The small one always suffers."

125

THE POOR, SUFFERING AND VERY FORGETFUL LITTLE COUNTRY AWARD...

Portugal – who'd been picked on so much they'd already been chosen as host country for Euro 2004!

Very happy ex-hosts

France, fresh from hosting and winning the World Cup in 1998, also became Euro champions in an amazing final. With just a minute of normal time to go they were losing! Then they equalized through striker Sylvain Wiltord and, in extra time, won the match with a golden goal from striker David Trezeguet.

France's winning goal was scored in the 13th minute of extra time, an unlucky number for some (opponents Italy thought so!) but not for France. Maybe the bad luck had been neutralized by their defender Lauren Blanc's pre-match superstition.

Furious Euro's question Just before the kick-off Blanc would kiss – what?
a) Something tall and wooden.
b) Something square and leathery.
c) Something round and skinny.
Answer: c) The round and shaven head of goalkeeper Fabien Barthez!

THE I'M SORRY, IT WAS ALL MY FAULT AWARD...

Shared by **the coaches of Germany, Holland, Italy and Portugal.** When their teams didn't win Euro 2000, they resigned.

EURO 2004

HOST COUNTRY: PORTUGAL

RUNNERS-UP: ?

WINNERS: ?

NO. OF TEAMS ENTERED: 50

NO. OF TEAMS IN FINAL: 16

The final sixteen

The qualifying rounds are over. Now it's time to assess the football form and decide who the Euro-stars will be this time round. Will England be effervescent? Greece grandiose? France frenetic? Denmark disparaging? Sweden swashbuckling and Switzerland swaggering? Latvia lachrymose? Bulgaria belligerent? Or will they all simply go out on the pitch and play some fantastic football? Here's your quick guide to the countries who will be in Portugal on the 12th of June for the start of the Euro 2004 finals.

Bulgaria (FIFA world ranking: 39)

How they got there: came top of Group 8 ahead of Croatia, Belgium, Estonia and Andorra.

Best group result: 3-0 v. Andorra.

Not-furious Euro-fact: Bulgaria will be pleased that Austria haven't qualified for Euro 2004 – in Bulgaria's first-ever international match in 1924 the Austrians whacked them 6-0!

Croatia (FIFA world ranking: 20)

How they got there: beat Slovenia 2-1 on aggregate in the play-offs after finishing second in Group 8.

Best group result: 4-0 v. Belgium.

Eye-wateringly furious Euro-fact: Wear sunglasses when Croatia are playing. During the 1998 World Cup, TV commentators complained because they couldn't read the Croatian player's names or numbers on their red-and-white checked shirts.

Czech Republic (FIFA world ranking: 10)
How they got there: came top of Group 3 ahead of Holland, Austria, Moldova and Belarus.
Best group result: 5-0 v. Moldova.
Possibly furious Euro-fact: The Czechs were unbeaten in their Euro 2004 group – which could be a bad sign. They started their Euro '96 group matches by giving lowly Luxembourg only their second win ever (1-0 to Luxembourg) ... but went on to reach the Euro '96 final.

Denmark (FIFA world ranking: 13)
How they got there: came top of Group 2 ahead of Norway, Romania, Bosnia-Herzegovina and Luxembourg.
Best group result: 5-2 away to Romania.
Wouldn't-be-at-all-furious Euro-fact: Denmark would just love to meet reigning champions France – so long as history repeats itself. In their first-ever international at the 1908 Olympic Games in London, the deadly Danes thumped the floundering French 9-0!

DENMARK ARE HOPING HISTORY REPEATS ITSELF

England (FIFA world ranking: 8)
How they got there: came top of
group 7 ahead of Turkey, Slovakia,
FYR Macedonia and Liechtenstein.
Best group result: 2-0 v. Turkey and
Liechtenstein (twice).
Furious Euro-players: the whole England
squad! When defender Rio Ferdinand was left out
of the side to meet Turkey in their deciding group
match (he'd failed to take a drugs test) the whole
squad threatened to go on strike! But in the end
they played and the game ended 0-0. In other
words, there weren't any strikes at all!

France (FIFA world ranking: 2)
How they got there: came top of
Group 1 ahead of Slovenia, Israel,
Cyprus and Malta.
Best group result: 6-0 v. Malta.
Furious Euro-fact: They're the reigning
European champions ... and if they win again the
other teams will be *furieux*!

130

Germany (FIFA world ranking: 9)
How they got there: came top of
Group 5 ahead of Scotland, Iceland,
Lithuania and Faroe Islands.
Best group result: 3-0 v. Iceland.
It-won't-seem-the-same-without-him furious
Euro-player: After Euro 2000, Germany's veteran
Lothar Matthaus finally retired. He'd won a world-
record 150 caps.

Greece (FIFA world ranking: 30)
How they got there: came top of
Group 6 ahead of Spain, Ukraine,
Armenia and Northern Ireland.
Best group result: 2-0 v. Armenia and Northern
Ireland.
Not-as-furious-as-they-thought-they-would-
be Euro-fact: After losing their first two group 6
games, Greece went on to win the remaining
6 without letting in a goal. In other words,
they turned a rough start into a Greece-y
smooth finish!

Holland (FIFA world ranking: 6)
How they got there: beat Scotland
6-1 on aggregate in the play-offs
after finishing second in Group 3.
Best group result: 5-0 v. Moldova ... then 6-0 v.
Scotland!
Was-furious-but-not-any-more Euro-player:
Ruud van Nistelrooy. When the Manchester
United striker was substituted during the group
match against Czech Republic, he booted a bottle,

spat on the ground and generally made it clear to coach Dick Advocaat that he wasn't happy. He was even less happy when he was left out for the next match. There were smiles all round at the end, though. Rampaging Ruud was brought back for the play-off against Scotland and banged in a hat-trick.

Italy (FIFA world ranking: 11)
How they got there: came top of Group 9 ahead of Wales, Serbia and Montenegro (that's one team), Finland and Azerbaijan.

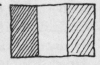

Best group result: 4-0 v. Azerbaijan and Wales.
Not-as-furious-as-I-looked Euro-player: star striker Christian Vieri, who threw a bottle at manager Giovanni Trapatonni when he was substituted. He said afterwards, "I didn't realize I had, the lads told me when they got into the changing rooms."

Latvia (FIFA world ranking: 56)

How they got there: beat Turkey 3-2 on aggregate in the play-offs after finishing second in Group 4.

Best group result: 3-0 v. San Marino.

Not-at-all furious Euro-fact: Euro 2004 is the first major tournament Latvia have ever qualified for. Coach Aleksandrs Starkovs said delightedly, "This is a great success for our nation." He was still smiling when the Latvian players grabbed him and threw him up in the air to celebrate their win!

Portugal (FIFA world ranking: 18)

How they got there: qualified automatically as hosts.

Furious Euro-fact: The Portuguese will be hoping to avoid next-door neighbours Spain. It was the sizzling Spaniards who gave Portugal one of their most embarrassing defeats: a 9-0 thumping in 1934.

Russia (FIFA world ranking: 29)

How they got there: beat Wales 1-0 on aggregate in the play-offs after finishing second in Group 10.

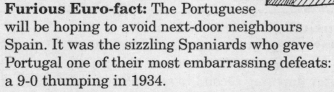

Best group result: 4-1 v. Albania and Switzerland.

Furious-or-frightened Euro-fact: After being held to a 0-0 draw in the first leg of their play-off, the Russians accused Wales' star player Ryan Giggs of elbowing one of their men ... and asked for him to be banned. The trick didn't work. Sadly, neither did Giggs. He hit the post, but Russia scored the only goal of the second game to reach the finals. Wales were left holding one record. They were the best-supported country in the whole qualifying tournament with a crowd of 73,000 cheering them on at almost every home game.

MAYBE WE'LL STAND A BETTER CHANCE THIS WAY !

Spain (FIFA world ranking: 3)

How they got there: beat Norway 5-1 on aggregate in the play-offs after finishing second in Group 6.

Best group result: 4-0 v. Armenia.

Furious-if-it-doesn't-happen-again Euro-fact: Spain will be hoping to meet Bulgaria in Euro 2004 – and match their record score. In 1933, the super Spaniards battered Bulgaria 13-0!

Sweden (FIFA world ranking: 17)

How they got there: came top of Group 4 ahead of Latvia, Poland, Hungary and San Marino.

Best group result: 6-0 v. San Marino.

Furious commentators Euro-fact: Sweden's squad is likely to have TV commentators crying into their microphones. For the Euro 2004 qualifying matches their players list included three Anderssons and three Svenssons – plus a Jonson, a Jonsson and a couple of Johanssons!

Switzerland (FIFA world ranking: 43)

How they got there: came top of Group 10 ahead of Russia, Republic of Ireland, Albania and Georgia.

Best group result: 4-1 v. Georgia.

Furious Euro-hosts fact: Switzerland will fancy their chances if they play the host country, Portugal. The only time they qualified was for Euro '96, when they opened the competition by holding hosts England to a 1-1 draw.

(Crystal) ball-watching!

So, who will win Euro 2004?

Which country will eu-tilise their players best and become Euro-champs?

Which will turn out to be the tournament's Euro-chumps?

If you're still undecided, here are some really eu-seless Euro-facts to help you make up your mind:

● The title has never been won with a team with a "B", "J", "Q" or "X" in their name.

● It's never been won by a team with 8, 9, 10, 12 or 13 letters in their name.

● It's never been won by a team from qualifying groups 2, 3, 9 or 10. (Group 10 isn't surprising; there'd never been a group 10 until Euro 2004 came along!)

So, with Azerbaijan ("B", "J", ten letters) already out, if history is to be made then it will have to be by the "B"-containing, 13-lettered, Group-3 winning CZECH REPUBLIC!

On the other hand...

● The title has been won most often by a team with the letter "A" in their name ... like FRANCE ...

● Which has most often had seven or 11 letters in its name ... like DENMARK or GERMANY...

● And most often qualified from group 7 ... like ENGLAND.

What's that? ENGLAND has seven letters as well? So it has. And it contains a letter "A"? That's amazing! Could it be that all the omens are pointing towards a historic win for England? Then maybe they should go flat out to really make a big impact on the record books. How? Obvious – by changing their name to BJQLAND in time for Euro 2004!

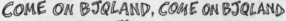

Fortunately, footballs rather than crystal balls are likely to play a more important part in Euro 2004. But, whatever actually happens you can be sure that, like all the contests in the past, Euro 2004 will have its share of the fantastic, the furious and the foul.

In other words, Euro 2004 will be business as eu-sual!

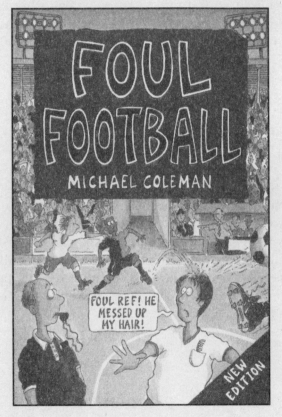

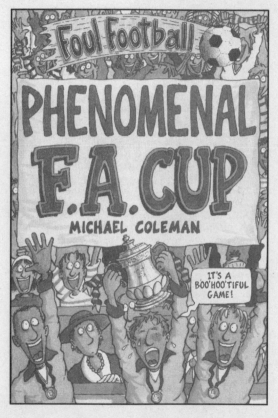

If you want to be in the game, get Foul Football!
Available now

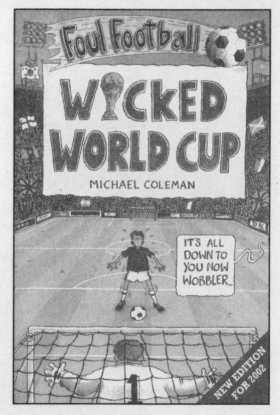

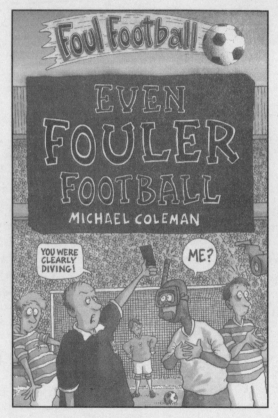

If you want to be in the game, get Foul Football!
Available August 2004